The Fullness of Being

THE
FULLNESS
OF
BEING

A New Paradigm for Existence

BARRY MILLER

UNIVERSITY OF NOTRE DAME PRESS

Notre Dame, Indiana

Paperback edition published in 2012

Library of Congress Cataloging-in-Publication Data
Miller, Barry, 1923–
The fullness of being : a new paradigm for existence / Barry Miller.
p. cm.
Includes bibliographical references and index.
ISBN 0-268-02864-4 (cloth : alk. paper)
ISBN 13: 978-0-268-03527-3 (pbk : alk. paper)
ISBN 10: 0-268-03527-X (pbk : alk. paper)
1. Ontology. I. Title.
BD311 .M55 2002
111'.1—dc21

2001004288

∞ The paper in this book meets the guidelines for permanence and durability
of the Committee on Production Guidelines for Book Longevity
of the Council on Library Resources.

Dedicated to the memory of

C. J. F. WILLIAMS,

fine philosopher and superb human being

Contents

Preface

According to a fairly standard view, there are various reasons that preclude existence from being a real property of concrete individuals. One such reason is that 'exists' cannot be predicated of individuals, and another is that first-level properties are parasitic on individuals for their actuality, which is something that existence could never be. A third is that, unlike all other real properties, existence would not add anything to an individual. Moreover, even if, per impossibile, existence were to survive all three counter-indications, it would be nothing but the most vacuous of properties.

These claims, however, are testimony to what happens when wrong questions are asked, when false assumptions are made, and when the possibility of a new paradigm for existence is not so much as entertained. In other words, they testify to the substantial flaws underlying the familiar claim 'Existence is not a predicate' and the Frege-Russell-Quine view not only of 'exists' as exclusively a second-level predicate but of existence as no more than a Cambridge property of individuals.

By way of contrast, the account in the following pages is a story of what happens when different questions are asked, when false assumptions are eschewed, and when the possibility of a radically different paradigm for existence is actively explored rather than completely ignored. It is a story that underlies acceptance of 'exists' as predicable of individuals, and of existence as the richest of an individual's properties, albeit far from invariant from individual to individual. Finally, it is a story that culminates in showing how perfectly good sense can be made of the notion 'the fullness of being.'

The book is dedicated to the late Christopher Williams, a friend who would have appreciated my gesture even if not my views. It belongs to what might loosely be called a 'trilogy', the other members of which are *From Existence to God* (1992) and *A Most Unlikely God* (1996). Characteristic of each is their selective drawing on some of the insights from Frege and Aquinas.

It is with deep gratitude that I acknowledge my debt not only to the comments of David Burrell and Brian Davies, but especially to detailed discussions with Peter Forrest, Mike Loux, and William Vallicella.

Barry Miller   All Saints Day, 2000
University of New England,
Australia

The Fullness of Being

one

The Question about 'Exists' and Existence

Like many philosophically interesting notions, existence is no less familiar than elusive. Although the verb 'exists' is as easy to use as the two-times table, it is no small feat to say just what it means for a concrete individual to exist.[1] Existing seems to be at least as mundane as walking or being hungry. Yet, when we say 'Tom is hungry' or 'Tom is walking,' it may be news to those not in Tom's vicinity, whereas 'Tom exists' would be news to no one who knew of Tom as a healthy human being, and merely puzzling to those who had never heard of him. Again, we can readily indicate what is meant by Tom's walking, but surely Tom's existence is not something we can indicate to anyone. On the face of it, we are greatly challenged to explain just what his existence is or what 'existence' means.

If we hearken to the voices of Russell and the late Christopher Williams, it is a challenge that we ignore at our peril, for Russell counsels that 'an almost unbelievable amount of false philosophy has arisen through not realizing what "existence" means.'[2] Presumably, his targets include such diverse philosophies as those of Parmenides, Plato, Aristotle, Aquinas, Heidegger, Paul Weiss, and

---

1. A concrete object can either cause or undergo change. An abstract object can do neither.

2. B. Russell, *Logic and Knowledge*, R. C. Marsh, ed. (London: Allen and Unwin, 1955), 234.

Milton Munitz,[3] to mention but a few, all of which fall in varying ways under the umbrella phrase 'philosophies of Being or Existence.' Williams dismisses them as 'paradigms of what Wittgenstein called man's bewitchment by language,' a bewitchment said to underlie the belief that 'the idea of existence is something deep and important, that existence is the central topic of philosophy.'[4] His distinguished work *What Is Existence?* seeks to exorcize those who have been thus bewitched. In it he offers readers an uncompromising apologia for the Frege-Russell view of existence, and in particular its twin claims that existence is not a property of individuals and that the expression 'exists' is not predicable of them. In so doing, his avowed aim is 'to destroy the foundations of an enormous amount of metaphysics.'[5]

Unconvinced by the Fregean thesis promoted by such as Russell, Quine, and Williams, I shall be arguing that the case for 'exists' being predicable of concrete objects is a product not of any bewitchment by language but of a distinctly more careful attention to language than Fregeans have been wont to give it. Before embarking on that task, however, it might be illuminating to reflect briefly not only on Frege's remarks on the existential use of 'exists' and 'is,' but on contributions from other sources as well.

I. Frege

In presenting Frege's views, I should mention that the existential use of 'is' is merely one of the four uses that he distinguished. Although

---

3. M. Munitz, *Existence and Logic* (New York: New York University Press, 1974). 'The chief problem of ontology . . . is to give a satisfactory account of existence' (204).

4. C. J. F. Williams, *What Is Existence?* (Oxford: Oxford University Press, 1981), ix. In similar vein, Simon Blackburn has suggested that 'a central mistake in this area is to treat Being as a particularly deep subject matter.' He has then given voice to the arresting, though unoriginal, view that 'this is parallel to treating Nothing as a name for a particular thing. . . .' *Dictionary of Philosophy* (Oxford: Oxford University Press, 1994), 4.

5. Ibid.

multiplicity of uses may or may not reflect any multiplicity of senses rather than merely differences of force, Frege had reasons for thinking that the four senses were not even systematically ambiguous or analogical, but had nothing at all in common. Each of the senses was borne by one or other of the four uses—by the 'is' of predication, of existence, of generic implication (class inclusion), and of identity, as illustrated below.

- The 'is' of *predication,* e.g., 'Socrates is wise,' rendered as 'Wise (Socrates)'.
- The *existential* 'is', e.g., 'Socrates is' and 'There are crocodiles,' the former being rendered in canonical language as '$(\exists x)(x =$ Socrates)', and the latter as '$(\exists x)(x$ is a crocodile).'
- The 'is' of *generic implication,* e.g., 'A crocodile is a reptile', rendered as '$(x)(\text{crocodile}(x) \supset \text{reptile}(x))$.'
- The 'is' of *identity,* e.g., 'Cicero is Tully,' rendered as 'Cicero = Tully.'

Although Frege clearly distinguishes the four uses, in no place does he group them all together. In one part the 'is' of (first-level) predication is distinguished from that of class inclusion, in another the 'is' of identity is distinguished from that of (first-level) predication, and in another the 'is' of existence is distinguished from that of (first-level) predication.[6] Fundamental to the distinctions are some of the now familiar Fregean doctrines concerning sense and reference, objects and concepts, and different levels of concepts, all being distinctions that I shall be employing in subsequent chapters. Objects are the referents of proper names which, for Frege, include all singular referring expressions; and concepts are the referents of predicates (concept expressions). According to Frege, a concept is not an intentional entity, as the term might have suggested. Rather, it is a property and is no less an ontological item than is an object, the

---

6. Predicates are first-level if they are said of individuals. They are second-level if they are said of properties of individuals.

difference being that properties (concepts) are incomplete entities whereas objects are complete.[7]

In an atomic proposition like 'Socrates is wise' the name 'Socrates' is to be distinguished from what is attached to it, namely, a predicate or concept expression. The name refers to an object and the predicate to a concept. A predicate that is said of an object is a first-level one. For Frege and Dummett, the name/predicate distinction is logically prior to the object/concept distinction, for objects are what names refer to, and concepts what predicates refer to, a point that I shall develop in chapter 3. Obviously, this is a much narrower use of 'object' and a much different use of 'concept' than we find in ordinary language.

In addition to first-level predicates there are higher-level ones. For example, the concept (property) referred to by the predicate 'is wise' is that of being wise or wisdom, and in 'Wisdom is rare' the predicate 'rare' is being said of that concept (property), for which reason it is called a second-level property or concept, and is the referent of a second-level predicate. There can of course be still higher-level predicates, with higher-level concepts as their referents.

These distinctions between objects and concepts (properties), and between first- and second-level predicates and first- and second-level concepts (properties) are basic to Frege's philosophical logic, and are a prerequisite for understanding some of his views on the uses of 'is'. As will now be evident, each use of 'is', except that of identity, bespeaks a radically different *relation* between those ontological items. The relation bespoken by the identity use is not between ontological items, however, but between linguistic ones—names. Below are the four relations.

1. The relation between *object* and (first-level) *concept:*
    Frege says that an object (Socrates) *falls under* a concept (wis-

---

7. The Fregean distinction between complete and incomplete *expressions* as well as between complete and incomplete *entities* is developed in chapter 3. For the moment, suffice it to say that objects are complete in that they can exist in their own right, whereas concepts (properties) are incomplete in that they can exist only as *of* (or belonging to) an object.

dom). This relation is expressed by the predicative use of 'is' in 'Socrates is wise'.

2. The relation between *concepts* of *different* levels, e.g., between first- and second-level concepts:

    Frege maintains that first-level concepts like wisdom *fall in* such second-level concepts as that of being rare. The relation is expressed by what he regards as the only way in which 'is' can be used existentially. For example, 'There are crocodiles' would be rendered as 'At least one thing is a crocodile' or '$(\exists x)(x$ is a crocodile)' in which the first-level concept of being a crocodile *falls in* the second-level concept referred to by the second-level predicate '$(\exists x)(x$ ___).'

3. The relation between *concepts* of the *same* level, e.g., between two first-level concepts:

    Socrates may *fall under* more than one first-level concept such as being a man, being rational, and being an animal. The latter two are said to be *subordinate* to the first concept because they are implicit in it. This relation is expressed by the 'is' of what has become known as 'class inclusion' or 'generic implication', as in 'A man is an animal.'

4. The relation between *names* of objects:

    At the beginning of Frege's *Über Sinn und Bedeutung* he asks whether identity is a relation between objects or between names of objects, and seems to have concluded that it was between names.[8] The relation is expressed by the 'is' of identity.

Frege on the Existential Use of 'Is'

For the purposes of this book, the only one of Frege's four uses of 'is' with which I shall be concerned is the existential one. Much of his treatment of it occurs in the 'Dialog mit Pünjer Über Existenz,'[9]

---

8. Wittgenstein argued that identity is not a relation at all, a view developed with some skill by C. J. F. Williams in his *What Is Identity?* (Oxford: Oxford University Press, 1989).

9. P. Long and R. White, eds., *Gottlob Frege: Posthumous Writings* (Oxford: Blackwell, 1979), 53–67.

which concludes with an illuminating exchange between him and Pünjer that does much to explain Frege's novel views on propositions[10] like 'Sachse exists' which to the philosophically untutored eye would seem unquestionably to be employing 'exists' as a first-level predicate and to be saying something about (Leo) Sachse.

Earlier in the discussion Frege had claimed that '"There are men" can be inferred from "Sachse is a man"'. To this Pünjer replied:

P. 'There are men' cannot be inferred from 'Sachse is a man' alone; you need the further sentence 'Sachse exists' as well.

F. My reply would be: If 'Sachse exists' is supposed to mean 'The word "Sachse" is not an empty sound, but designates something,' then it is true that the condition 'Sachse exists' must be satisfied.[11] But this is not a new premise, but the presupposition of all our words—a presupposition that the words we use are not empty, that our sentences express judgements, that one is not playing a mere game with words. Once 'Sachse is a man' expresses an actual judgement, the word 'Sachse' must designate something, and in that case I do not need a further premise in order to infer 'There are men' from it. The premise 'Sachse exists' is redundant, if it is to mean something different from the above-mentioned presupposition of all our thinking.

---

10. In using the term 'proposition' here and throughout the book, I do *not* intend it to refer to any abstract entity. Rather, it is to refer to a linguistic entity considered quite independently of whether it is being asserted, stated, or simply proposed for consideration. For example, neither 'p' nor 'q' in 'if p then q' is being asserted or stated, but is merely being enunciated. In other contexts, of course, p and q may well be used with assertoric or even interrogative force. When, however, I do intend to refer not to such a linguistic entity but to some supposedly abstract entity, I shall use a capital 'P' as in 'Proposition.'

11. I might interject to note that this is only half true. The condition that must be satisfied is not merely 'Sachse exists' but 'Sachse exists *or has existed.*'

According to Frege, therefore, 'Leo Sachse exists' is unnecessary because all proper names must be supposed to have a bearer: 'exists' says nothing about the person Leo Sachse. It does, however, say something about the expression 'Leo Sachse,' namely, that the term designates something. But, says Frege, because it 'predicates something self-evident . . . it really has no content' (p. 62).

Pünjer maintains that, even if the self-evidence of singular existential propositions disqualifies them from having any content, the same point is inapplicable to particular existential propositions like 'Some men exist' which are certainly not self-evident. Since that proposition is rendered in German by 'Es gibt Menschen,' Frege has no difficulty in pointing out that its content cannot be attributed to any existential verb. (The point for English speakers is simply that 'es gibt' is not to be translated as 'exists' but as 'there is.') Wherein, then, does its content lie? Frege explains that the 'real content of what is predicated [lies] . . . in the form of the particular judgement' (p. 64). Thus, 'exist' in particular propositions has no more content than in singular propositions, though for different reasons. Further insight into what he means by saying that 'exists' has no content but is merely the form of a proposition is given in *Die Grundlagen der Arithmetik,* where he explains in §53 that 'the proposition that there exists no rectangular equilateral rectilinear triangle does state a property of the concept "rectangular equilateral rectilinear triangle"; it assigns to it the number nought.' Then follows the familiar sentence:

Affirmation of existence is in fact nothing but denial of the number nought.

This means, as he says in *Über Sinn und Bedeutung,* that 'existence is a property of a concept,' i.e., it is merely a second-level property. On this understanding, therefore, propositions like 'There are pygmies' are to be understood as composed of the first-level concept expression '___ is a pygmy' and the second-level concept expression '$(\exists x)(x$ ___).' Understood in this way, 'There are pygmies' tells us that more than zero objects fall under the concept *being a pygmy*. And, if 'Leo Sachse exists' is to have any sense at all, it is to be understood as composed in precisely the same way. A first-level concept expression (viz. '___ is identical with Leo Sachse') is combined with the second-level expression '$(\exists x)(x \underline{\quad})$' to form '$(\exists x)(x =$ Leo Sachse)' or, in nonsymbolic terms, 'There is at least one thing that is identical with Leo Sachse.'[12] Thus interpreted, it is clear that nothing is being predicated of Leo Sachse. Rather, something is being said about the property (or concept) of being identical with Leo Sachse: we are being told how often that particular property is instantiated, namely, at least once. And, of course, 'at least once' is 'the denial of nought.'

There might now seem to be good grounds for identifying Frege's relation of *falling under* as the relation of instantiating or exemplifying. Williams, however, reminds us that 'There are pygmies' would entail 'The concept of being a pygmy is instantiated at least once.' The difficulty with this is that Frege regards 'the concept of being a pygmy' as a proper name and thus as referring to an object, if it refers to anything. The suggested translation would therefore entail 'An object is instantiated at least once,' which is quite impossible, for an essential mark of objects (as distinct from Fregean concepts) is precisely that they are not instantiable at all.

As both Geach and Dummett have noted,[13] when discussing the problem posed by the expression 'the concept horse,' the difficulty can readily be overcome by using a 'what'-clause rather than the singular term 'the concept of being a pygmy.' It is entirely proper to say 'What the predicate "is a pygmy" refers to is instantiated at least once'—provided we recognize that the 'what'-clause is being used as a *first*-level *predicable* to which is attached the *second*-level predicate 'is instantiated at least once.' In canonical language, the proposition would be '$(\exists x)(x$ is what "is a pygmy" refers to).'

To sum up. In regard to the existential use of 'is', Frege takes himself to have made two points, one ontological (about existence) and the other logical (about 'exists').

- The ontological point is that there is no room for existence as a first-level property. In any ostensibly singular existential propo-

---

12. As we shall see, this is the proposal adopted later by Quine.

13. M. Dummett, *Frege, Philosophy of Language*, 2nd ed. (London: Duckworth, 1981), 213–14. G. E. M. Anscombe and P. T. Geach, *Three Philosophers* (Oxford: Blackwell, 1969), 155–56.

sition like 'Leo Sachse exists,' the expression 'exists' predicates nothing of Leo Sachse. The proposition is not about the individual Leo Sachse but about the name 'Leo Sachse,' or about the property of being identical with Leo Sachse.

• The logical point is that there is no room for 'exists' as a first-level predicate. Whether in 'Leo Sachse exists' or in 'Some men exist,' 'exists' always functions as a second-level predicate, and what it stands for is a property of a concept, namely, the (second-level) property of having at least one object falling under it. 'Some men exist' is saying that *being a man* has more than zero objects falling under it. 'Leo Sachse exists' is saying that *being identical with Leo Sachse* has more than zero objects falling under it.[14]

Attempted Amendments to Frege

On the face of it, Frege's contention that 'Leo Sachse exists' is about the name 'Leo Sachse' is distinctly implausible. Both Russell and Quine were later to suggest apparently more plausible alternatives. Their common strategy was to treat the name 'Leo Sachse' as eminently dispensable. Russell did so by replacing it with a definite description. Thus, the name 'Socrates' was to be replaced by the description 'the teacher of Plato,' thereby allowing 'Socrates exists' to be rendered as 'The teacher of Plato exists.' This could then be transformed into 'Exactly one thing is a teacher of Plato,' a proposition which did not have even the appearance of being about Socrates. Quine's proposal was to embrace the second of Frege's own suggestions and to render 'Socrates exists' as 'Something is identical with Socrates,' which in turn was to be transformed into 'Something socratizes.' This, too, seemed not to be about Socrates. Using these devices, Russell and Quine could perhaps be regarded as having put the finishing touches to Frege's proposal for eliminating any first-level use of 'exists,' and to have done so without accepting his severely

---

14. *Pace* Williams, I might add that 'falls under' can indeed be rendered as 'instantiates.'

strained interpretation of 'Leo Sachse exists' as being about a name. Both attempts were well intentioned. Whether they were successful will be discussed in chapter 2.

The view propagated by Frege, Russell, and Quine—that 'exists' in Socrates exists' says absolutely nothing about Socrates—is one that I shall call the 'redundancy' theory of 'exists.'[15] These three were not, however, pioneers of the theory for, as I shall now explain, it had been held in less developed form by Aristotle, Hume, and Kant, all of whom reached much the same conclusion, though for different reasons.

II. OTHER REDUNDANCY VIEWS

Aristotle (384–322 B.C.): His position on the existential 'is' is quite clear. As G. E. L. Owens reminds us, Aristotle takes 'to be' to mean 'to be so-and-so.'[16] For Socrates to be is for him to be what he is, i.e., what he essentially is. If Socrates is essentially a man, then for Socrates to be would be for him to be a man. 'Socrates is' would therefore be simply elliptical for 'Socrates is so-and-so,' where the permissible substitutions for 'so-and-so' would be any of Socrates' essential predicates. On this view, 'is' would be quite unambiguous because its use would always be predicative, either explicitly as in 'Socrates is a man' or merely elliptically as in 'Socrates is.' Nowhere does Aristotle distinguish the two uses that Geach was later to call the 'actuality' and 'there is' senses. It is because Aristotle allows an apparently existential use of 'is' to be reduced to a predicative use that I call him a redundancy theorist.

Turning now from Aristotle on 'is' to Aristotle on existence, we might note his conclusion in the *Metaphysics* that, for any entity to

---

15. The redundancy theory might also be described as treating propositions of the form '*a* exists' as always reducible to a form that contains no first-level use of 'exists' or 'is.' The non-redundancy theory denies the possibility of any such reduction.

16. G. E. L. Owens, 'Aristotle on the Snares of Ontology' in R. Bambrough, *New Essays on Plato and Aristotle* (London: Routledge and Kegan Paul, 1965), 69–96. See also M. Loux, *Primary Ousia* (Ithaca: Cornell University Press, 1991), chap. 1.

be, was for it to be what it is, i.e., what it essentially is. If Socrates is essentially a man, then for him to be would be for him to be a man. So, the *immediate* explanation of the reality of Socrates would be in terms of his being a man. One might then ask what would explain the reality of being a man, with the answer being that it would stem from being an animal, and so on. At each point, the explanation of Socrates' existence would be in terms of what it is essentially. The point would be reached, however, when the explanation would be in terms of the category to which he belongs, which is substance. But this could not be the ultimate explanation of his reality, since the same question could be asked of substance.

Now, if being were itself a genus, then substance might belong to it. This option, however, is not open to Aristotle, since he insisted that being is not a genus. So, although for Socrates to be is for him to be what he is essentially, we can pursue that lead as far as we wish, but will never reach the point at which being (existence) is part of the essence of any genus. As Aristotle recognized, Socrates' reality would ultimately have to be demonstrated. This, however, should not be taken as tacit recognition that existence is some kind of ontological element additional to Socrates, for he says quite explicitly that 'one man and a man are the same thing, and existent man and a man are the same thing, and the doubling of the words in "one man" and "one existent man" does not give any new meaning (it is clear that they are not separated either in coming to be or ceasing to be).'[17]

In regard to existence, therefore, Aristotle was no less a redundancy theorist than he was in regard to the use of 'is' as a predicate of individuals.

Hume (1711–76): For reasons peculiar to his own impression-based epistemology, Hume argued that 'the idea of existence must either be derived from a distinct impression, conjoined with every perception or object of our thought, or must be the very same with the idea of the perception or object.'[18] There being nothing to indicate the presence of any impression that is 'conjoined with every

---

17. *Metaphysics*, Book Γ 1003ᵇ 26–29,
18. D. Hume, *Treatise of Human Nature,* bk. I, part II, sec. vi.

perception or object of our thought,' he concludes that there is no distinct impression from which the idea of existence could be derived. Anyone dissenting from this view would, suggests Hume, be obliged to indicate just what distinct impression was correlative to the idea of existence.[19]

Finally, Hume tells us that 'the idea of existence, then, is the very same with the idea of what we conceive to be existent. To reflect on anything simply and to reflect on it as existent, are nothing different from each other. That idea, when conjoined with the idea of any object, makes no addition to it.' In other words, the role of existence is redundant. His contention that the idea of existence 'makes no addition' to the idea of any object is reminiscent of Aristotle. It was to be reaffirmed in Kant, not to mention in many of our contemporaries including Russell and Quine, to whose views I shall return in chapter 2.

Kant (1724–1804): Though not espousing Hume's impressionism, Kant's view of existence was not far removed from the conclusion drawn by Hume, as evidenced by the following familiar passage:

> By whatever and by however many predicates we may think a thing—even if we completely determine it—we do not make the least addition to the thing when we further declare that this thing is. . . . If we think in a thing every feature of reality except one, the missing reality is not added by my saying that this defective thing exists.[20]

---

19. Somewhat similar was Berkeley's view that there is no abstract idea of existence nor even a particular idea, since it is not a color, smell, taste, sound or feeling. B. Berkeley, *The Philosophical Commentaries*, A. A. Luce ed. (London: Nelson, 1944), 671.

20. I. Kant, *Critique of Pure Reason*, B628. In B627, however, Kant had acknowledged that his financial position was 'affected very differently by a hundred real thalers than it is by the mere concept of them (that is, of their possibility). For the object, as it actually exists, is not analytically contained in my concept, but is added to my concept (which is a determination of my state) synthetically.'

Earlier he had claimed that 'the real contains no more than the merely possible. A hundred real thalers do not contain the least coin more than a hundred possible thalers.'[21]

Not surprisingly, therefore, he was well able to maintain that '"being" is not a real predicate,' though he does allow that it is a logical one, for 'anything we please can be made to serve as a logical predicate.' Logically, however, 'it is merely the copula of a judgment.'[22] In the light of Frege's subsequent insight that the copula was entirely dispensable, it is not difficult for us to recognize the logic of Kant's refusal to allow 'being' the status of a real predicate.[23]

That being so, just what role does he think 'is' plays in such propositions as 'God is' or 'God is omnipotent'? In both cases, says Kant, its role is simply to posit (*setzen*) the subject. In the former, it posits the subject (God) 'in itself with all its predicates'; in the latter it posits the predicate in relation to the subject (God).[24] The 'is' in the former and the 'is' in the latter seem to be merely two uses of the one notion.

III. NON-REDUNDANCY VIEWS

From even so sketchy a survey it is reasonably clear that the redundancy view of 'exists' and existence has held sway for much of the history of philosophy. In the Middle Ages, however, some prominent figures were firmly of the opposite view. Among the Arabs were Al-farabi and Avicenna (Ibn Sina), among the Europeans were Aquinas, Henry of Ghent, and Godfrey of Fontaines. There were many others. Despite differing on many points, they were agreed in recognizing

---

21. Ibid., B627.

22. Ibid., B626. See also B627: 'The small word "is" adds no new predicate, but only serves to posit the predicate *in its relation to* the subject. . . . The content of both must be one and the same; nothing can have been added to the concept, which expresses merely what is possible, by my thinking its object (through the expression "it is") as given absolutely.'

23. Ibid., B627.

24. Ibid.

that an individual was sharply to be distinguished from existence, which was by no means redundant. I shall briefly note some of their pertinent points.

Avicenna (960–1037): Together with Averroes (1126–1196), Avicenna was one of the pre-eminent Arabian philosophers of the Middle Ages. However, I mention him because, unlike Aristotle, whom he admired, he did insist on existence having an ontological role that was quite distinct from that of essence and certainly not redundant.[25] Essences, he noted, can be present both in things as well as (intentionally) in the intellect. In the former case they are engaged in the reality of things, in the latter they are conceived of by the intellect. If it were essential to them that they be particular, they could never be in intellect; and if it were essential to them that they be universal, they could never be in things. Considered in se, therefore, they were in neither. In se they were neither universal nor particular, but merely could be either.

Avicenna's recognition of a real role for existence presented him with a problem, for if an essence had no actuality in its own right, there would be nothing to which its existence could accrue. This is a difficulty that must be faced and resolved by any theory that allows existence a real ontological role. Avicenna's particular solution was to deny one term of the problem by accepting that an essence was *not* totally devoid of actuality in its own right but did have a certain kind of existence which Henry of Ghent was later to name 'esse essentiae' (the being or existence of an essence), albeit an existence that was much inferior to actual existence (*esse existentiae*). Although the distinction between *esse essentiae* and *esse existentiae* might strike us as highly fanciful, it is hardly more fanciful than that between existing and being actual that is employed in some contemporary haecceity theories.

Avicenna's essences entered the realm of the actual only when existence (*esse existentiae*) accrued (*accidit*) to them. As he noted,

---

25. Avicenna, *The Healing*, first treatise, chap. 6, translated by A. Hyman in A. Hyman and J. J. Walsh, eds., *Philosophy in the Middle Ages* (Indianapolis: Hackett, 1974), 240–62.

'this existence, far from being an accident, i.e., being posterior to and pre-supposing an essence, is, in fact, anterior to essence and pre-supposed by it.'[26]

Henry of Ghent (d. 1293): Since there is much in common between Henry and Avicenna, I shall discuss him before Aquinas, who lived before him. Like Avicenna, Henry distinguished between an individual and its existence. He argued that, considered in se, essences were objects of God's knowledge, and hence must have some kind of being or existence, which he called *esse essentiae*. As he puts it, insofar as such entities exist as objects of God's knowledge, their being is not so minimal that they are not also something in themselves.[27] Being something in se—independently of *esse existentiae*—they are the entities to which actual existence (*esse existentiae*) might be said to accrue.

I have chosen to discuss Avicenna and Henry of Ghent not out of any antiquarian interest, but because they highlight one possible way of responding to the puzzle that is inevitable once a distinction is drawn between an individual and its existence. The puzzle is this:

> Socrates' existence belongs to Socrates no less than does his wisdom. Because Socrates without his wisdom would not be devoid of actuality, there is something to which his wisdom can be said to belong or accrue. But the same cannot be said of his existence, for Socrates without his existence would be totally devoid of actuality, i.e., Socrates would have no actuality in his own right. How could existence be said to belong to something that had no actuality in its own right?

Although Avicenna, Henry of Ghent, and Aquinas each regarded Socrates as parasitic on his existence in respect of actuality, it was only the first two who offered any explanation as to how an instance

---

26. F. Rahman, 'Essence and Existence in Ibn Sina, the Myth and the Reality', *Hamdard Islamicus* 4 (1981): 6.

27. *Quodlibet*, 9. Cited by J. Wippel in his *Metaphysical Themes in Thomas Aquinas* (Washington, D.C.: Catholic University of America Press, 1984), 177.

of existence could be said to accrue to a Socrates that had no actuality in its own right. They tried to resolve the difficulty by allowing
that it could do so through the medium of the essence of man, which
they maintained did have some actuality in its own right, namely,
esse essentiae. It is this entity, then, to which *esse existentiae* was supposed to accrue.

Aquinas (1225–74): It was one thing to recognize existence as
an ontologcal constituent of any existent, as Avicenna and Henry
did, but quite another to accept the notion of *esse essentiae*. Aquinas
rejected that notion. He did, however, accept that an individual's
instance of existence was by no means redundant, and was sharply
to be distinguished from the individual to which it belonged. He accepted, too, that existence was logically prior to essence, and hence
not an accident. The onus, however, was on him to explain just
what the relation might be between an individual and its instance
of existence, given that the latter could not be an accident. It was
an onus that, so far as I can see, he seems not to have discharged,
as I explain in note 21 of chapter 4. This problem is inevitable for
anyone distinguishing between an individual and its instance of
existence. It is also the central problem in this book, but one which
will be shown in chapter 4 to be by no means insoluble—even while
eschewing Avicenna's strategy of denying one term of the problem.

If we move now from the ontological to the linguistic plane and
Aquinas' views on 'is,' it has to be said that they are not concentrated
in any one of his works but are scattered through many of them.
Fortunately, however, they have been assembled and interrelated in
an illuminating study by Hermann Weidemann.[28] Like Aristotle,
Aquinas had no difficulty in distinguishing the existential use of 'is'
from the 'is' of identity and the 'is' of predication.[29] It has also to be
said that he regarded the last two as closely related, with the predicative use being marked by an element of identity, and the identity
use by an element of predication. He distinguished, however, be-

---

28. H. Weidemann, 'The Logic of Being in Thomas Aquinas,' in
S. Knuuttila and J. Hintikka, eds., *The Logic of Being* (Dordrecht: Reidel,
1985), 181–200.

29. *Summa Theologica*, I, q.39, a.5.

tween two existential uses of 'is.'[30] In one of them, 'is' is taken to express the being of whatever falls under the Aristotelian categories, whether the being of a substance or that of its accidents. As used in this way, 'is' refers to that by which something is actual. In the second existential sense, however, it expresses the truth of a proposition. Following Geach, these two existential uses might be called the 'actuality' and the 'there-is' uses respectively.[31] As expressed in contemporary terms, this is the distinction between 'is' or 'exists' as first-level predicates on the one hand and as second-level predicates on the other. It runs directly counter to Frege's redundancy view that the sole existential use is a second-level one.

IV. Issues Yet to Be Addressed

In the preceding pages I have not tried to provide anything like an exhaustive account of the views on 'exists' and existence that Western philosophers have held over the last two and a half millennia. Perhaps, however, I have done enough to illustrate the enormity of the divide between two camps. On the one hand are the majority of philosophers for whom a first-level use of 'exists' and a first-level property of existence are both redundant. On the other hand is the much smaller group in the Middle Ages, and some even today, for whom neither is redundant. Their belief in a first-level use of 'exists' and a first-level property of existence is held with no less conviction than is the dictum 'Existence is not a predicate' by the majority group. Although weight of numbers is far from decisive, one might be forgiven for wondering what room could remain for discussion on these matters. Why exhume them now? Surely they should be

---

30. *Quodlibet,* IX, q.2, a.2.

31. These terms were introduced in P. T. Geach, 'What Actually Exists,' *Proceedings of the Aristotelian Society,* supp. vol. 42 (1968), reprinted in his *God and the Soul* (London: Routledge and Kegan Paul, 1969). See also his account of Aquinas on existence in *Three Philosophers,* 90–91, where he argues that 'Aquinas' conception of *esse* depends on there being a sense of the verb *"est"* or "is" quite other than the "there is" sense.' Emphasis in the original.

allowed to rest in peace. I am inclined to think not, and shall be pressing that point in succeeding chapters.

The first and unquestionably fundamental issue to be pressed is whether the Fregean view of 'exists' as invariably a second-level predicate is correct. If so, that would be the end of the story. Unless Frege can be shown to be mistaken on this point, it would be quixotic in the extreme to take up the cudgels on behalf of a first-level property of existence and all the questions that would issue therefrom. However, I think that the Fregean view is misguided, and that a very strong case indeed can be made for 'exists' having a first-level use. That, in fact, will be the purport of the next chapter, in which I confront the Fregean view, resolve the paradoxes and absurdities which the non-redundancy view has been accused of generating, and expose some of the misconceptions embodied in the Fregean view itself.

While that chapter is undoubtedly the linchpin of the whole enterprise, it is only the beginning. To show that 'exists' is a first-level predicate is of course to have shown also that its referent (existence) is a first-level property. That, however, does not take us very far, for it still leaves open the possibility of existence being a merely Cambridge property.[32] I shall argue in chapter 3 that it is in fact a real property. To establish that point is inevitably to open a veritable can of worms, for immediately we are confronted with the problem to which I alluded in discussing Avicenna, Henry of Ghent, and Aquinas. It is the problem of how on earth Socrates could have any actuality if his actuality were due solely to his instance of existence—and if that instance were logically *prior* to him.

---

32. The term 'Cambridge property' is simply an extension of Geach's use of 'Cambridge change.' According to Russell, there is a change between times t_1 and t_2 if the truth-value at t_1 differs from the truth-value at t_2. On that criterion, however, my being thought of by someone else would be no less a change in *me* than my being wounded. Clearly they are vastly different, and not merely in degree. Geach has coined the term 'Cambridge change' to distinguish the former from the latter, which is a real change. I have simply extended the application of the adjective 'Cambridge' from changes to properties as well. My being observed by someone would be a Cambridge property, whereas my being wounded by someone would be a real one.

There is no comparable problem in regard to his other properties, like his instance of wisdom, for it is quite clear that Socrates is already 'there' logically prior to receiving them. The same cannot be said, however, for his instance of existence: logically prior to his instance of existence, he cannot have any actuality whatever, and hence cannot be 'there' to receive his instance of existence. This presents comparatively little difficulty for Avicenna and Henry of Ghent for they are able to point to essences in se (having *esse essentiae*) as recipients of actual existence (*esse existentiae*). But that proposal is no help to people like Aquinas who would regard *esse essentiae* as nothing but an ontological extravagance, or perhaps even a *deus ex machina,* on the part of its proponents. Once *esse essentiae* is dismissed, as it should be, the resolution of this problem calls for a deal of lateral thinking including a paradigm shift in our notion of existence, details of which I shall leave for chapter 4. The solution will also provide answers to such familiar questions as 'If existence is a real property of individuals, what does it add to them?' or 'How can existence be a property of individuals, if it adds nothing to them?'

There are yet other questions to be answered. One of them queries the ontological wealth of instances of existence. Surely, it will be urged, if an instance of existence is had by everything from a subatomic particle to Aristotle and Einstein, it must be among the 'thinnest' of all property instances. As a consequence of the notion of existence arrived at in chapter 4, instances of existence will be recognized as the sufficient condition not only for an individual's being something rather than nothing, but also for his being a man rather than a mouse, wise rather than unwise, and intelligent rather than unintelligent. As well, the wealth of the instances of existence will be seen to vary considerably from individual to individual.

Finally, there will be the question of whether any sense could be made of an instance of existence that would be the apogee of ontological wealth, one that might justly be said to enjoy the 'fullness of being.' My answer will be 'yes,' and I shall be at pains to explain just what such an entity would be like.

Let me now close this introductory chapter by offering an overview of what lies ahead.

- The sine qua non is to determine whether the redundancy theorists are right in denying 'exists' any use as a predicate of concrete individuals. I shall be arguing at length in chapter 2 that they are mistaken. 'Exists' is a first-level predicate, and hence existence is a first-level property.
- The immediate question then is 'What kind of property, Cambridge or real?' It would have been hardly surprising had it been a Cambridge property, but in chapter 3 that is just what it will prove not to be.
- That conclusion, however, might seem positively counter-intuitive since first-level properties—at least those other than existence—are logically posterior to individuals, whereas existence is logically prior to them. How can that be? In the event, it will prove possible to reconcile the apparently irreconcilable by finding a way in which an instance of existence can be logically prior to an individual—without casting any doubt on its bona fides as a property instance. The solution in chapter 4 will be that an individual is not the subject in which its instance of existence inheres, but is that which bounds its instance of existence.
- Apart from proposing a paradigm shift in our notion of existence, this relation will have significant implications for instances of existence. For one thing, although it has been customary to ask what an instance of existence might add to an individual, this will be exposed as a question that might sensibly be asked only of a property that was logically *posterior* to individuals (inhered in them), but cannot even sensibly be asked of any property instance (existence) that is logically *prior* to an individual in respect of actuality.
- It has also been customary to think that, even if there were instances of existence, their role would be limited strictly to that in virtue of which an individual is something rather than nothing. Because an instance of existence is *bounded* by an individual, however, that cannot be its only one. In fact, in chapter 5 it will prove to be also that in virtue of which an individual is both the *kind* of entity it is and has each of the *property instances* that it does have.
- That, too, has some interesting implications, for it will dispose not only of the idea that an instance of existence is the most im-

poverished of property instances but also of the quaint idea that Aristotle's or Einstein's instances of existence carry no more ontological weight than that of a quark or an electron.

- Since the ontological wealth of Aristotle's instance of existence so far exceeds that of a quark, it would be interesting to know just how far even the wealth of Aristotle's instance of existence might be exceeded, at least in principle. The answer to this question will be found in chapter 6, which will also show the vanity of Christopher Williams' ambition to destroy the foundations of an enormous amount of metaphysics.

All of these anticipated conclusions will remain simply pie in the sky until it has been shown that Frege was wrong about 'exists,' and hence that there is no truth to the dictum 'Existence is not a Predicate.' The task of the next chapter will be to do just that.

two

'Exists' as Predicable of Concrete Individuals

Christopher Williams rightly remarked that 'almost everything that has been said by philosophers about existence is the result of their treating "is" or "exist" as a predicate of objects.'[1] As we have seen, much current thinking—with such notable exceptions as Geach,[2] Mackie,[3] and Evans[4]—is that 'exists' can never be predicated of individuals, and that its existential use is exhausted by its role as a second-level predicate. This is often summed up by latter-day disciples of Frege and Russell in the familiar dictum, 'Existence is not a predicate.'[5] A corollary of such a view is that existence could not be a property of individuals. The main point of this chapter is to show that neither contention can be sustained.

---

1. C. J. F. Williams, *What Is Existence?* (Oxford: Oxford University Press, 1981), ix.

2. P. T. Geach, 'What Actually Exists,' *Proceedings of the Aristotelian Society,* supp. vol. 42 (1968): 7–16. Reprinted in his *God and the Soul* (London: Routledge and Kegan Paul, 1969), chap. 5.

3. J. L. Mackie, 'The Riddle of Existence,' *Proceedings of the Aristotelian Society,* supp. vol. 50 (1976): 247–67.

4. G. Evans, *The Varieties of Reference* (Oxford: Oxford University Press, 1982), chap. 10.

5. This would be expressed more accurately either by '"Exists" is not a (first-level) predicate' or by 'Existence is not a (first-level) property.'

How does one argue that 'exists' can be predicated of individuals? Seemingly, nothing could be better than to produce clear-cut cases of precisely such predications. 'Socrates exists,' 'Socrates no longer exists' or 'Socrates is no more,'[6] and 'Socrates might never have existed' have been suggested as prime examples of just that,[7] as have the biblical examples 'Joseph is not and Simeon is not' and 'Before Abraham was, I am.' I cite the biblical propositions not for the quality of their translation, but for the quality of their English. In fact, at least one of them is a very poor translation. However, even if the translators were not masters of their craft, they have long been recognized as masters of the English tongue. Hence, whatever aspersions might be cast on the accuracy of their translations, there can be no doubt that they were expressed in impeccable English, including their first-level uses of 'exists.'

But what if all are dismissed as being highly misleading, and capable of being so rephrased as to contain no evidence of 'exists' being predicated of Socrates or of anything else? In that case, there would be little option but to embark on the negative strategy of assessing in turn each of the putative reasons for not taking the prima facie examples at face value after all. If such reasons proved consistently defective, the stage would ultimately be reached when it would be pointless trying to force all uses of 'exists' into the procrustean bed of second-level predication rather than accept the aforementioned propositions[8] for precisely what they purport to be, namely, predications made of Socrates, Joseph, Simeon, or Jesus Christ as the case may be. This is the course I shall be following.

Part I will be concerned primarily with objections based on the absurdities and paradoxes that are said to be the inevitable upshot of denying existence to concrete individuals. This is the so-called

---

6. 'Arrowby is no more' is another example, mentioned by G. E. L. Owen in his 'Aristotle on the Snares of Ontology,' in R. Bambrough, ed., *New Essays on Plato and Aristotle* (London: Routledge and Kegan Paul, 1965), 71.

7. In addition, Mackie, 'Riddle of Existence,' has suggested 'John does not know that this beach exists.'

8. Remember that by 'proposition' I mean a linguistic entity, not an abstract one.

problem of negative existential propositions, and it dominates the case against any first-level use of 'exists.' Then, in Part II, I shall argue against various other reasons that have been advanced with the same intent.

I. Putative Absurdity and Paradox of Negative Existential Propositions

As noted in the preceding chapter, Frege argued that 'There are subjects of which being must be denied' would mean 'Something that has being falls under the concept of not-being.' This, he contends, is a difficulty from which there is no escape 'once a content of some kind . . . is agreed to the concept of being.' In other words, if 'exists' had any content at all, then the denial of existence as in 'Socrates does not exist' would have the embarrassing consequence of generating the contradiction 'Socrates who has being has no being.' Since this is said to ensue no matter what content is ascribed to 'exists,' the suggested conclusion must, of course, be that 'exists' has just no content at all. Frege's objection is thus closely related to the paradoxes and absurdities that many more recent philosophers are apt to regard as generated by negative singular existential propositions.

The supposed absurdity derives from the claim that if existence were a property, then nonexistence would be one also. And that would give rise to such zany situations as sheep farmers inspecting their flocks daily 'with the aim of sorting the existing sheep from the non-existent ones—searching for the stigmata of existence'[9] and of horticulturists examining 'several specimens of blue buttercup before concluding that none of them exist.'[10]

As for the paradox alleged to be generated by negative existential propositions, it arises in this way. If 'exists' is a predicate, then its negation should be a predicate also. But if 'does (do) not exist' is a predicate, then in 'Dragons do not exist' it is predicated of dragons.

---

9. D. G. Londey, 'Existence,' *Philosophia Arhusiensis* 1 (1970): 3.

10. C. J. F. Williams, *Being, Identity, and Truth* (Oxford: Oxford University Press, 1992), 1.

But it can be predicated of dragons only if dragons do exist. And similarly for all general negative existential propositions—paradoxically, if 'does not exist' is to be predicated at all, it can be predicated only of what *does* exist. Nor are singular propositions like 'Lord Hailsham does not exist' said to fare any better. Despite his demise, there are of course true predications that can still be made about Lord Hailsham—that he was a politician, that he was an aristocrat, and the like. 'Does not exist' could be true of him only after there was any Lord Hailsham for it to be true of. So, precisely the same paradox arises with Lord Hailsham as with dragons.

Since Christopher Williams has presented arguably the most thoroughgoing discussion of 'exists' and existence, I shall follow him as he argues not only that there is a genuine paradox but that its solution is to recognize that 'exists' is merely a second-level predicable and, indeed, that the second-level account is the only one 'that does justice to the various requirements of our thought.'[11] Beginning with 'Blue buttercups exist,' he observes that there is no reason to accept that 'exists' is being predicated of buttercups, for what we want to say can be expressed equally well by 'Some buttercups are blue.' Tellingly, however, this makes no mention of existence: all it affirms is that there are such things as blue buttercups, and all we are denying is that no buttercups are blue.

On the basis of this contention he suggests that perhaps it was absurd to think that 'existence, or being is a property shared by black swans, good arguments for increased public spending, and ways of cooking eggs without breaking their shells, despite the fact that there *are* black swans, there *are* good arguments for increased public spending, there *are* ways of cooking eggs without breaking their shells.'[12] What, then, is going on when we say 'Blue buttercups exist'? He suggests that the proposition is a response to the question 'How many blue buttercups are there?' to which the answer is that there are 'some' (one or more). This leads him to conclude that 'exists' is being used to express number in much the same way as do terms like 'abound' or 'rare' or 'numerous.'

---

11. Ibid., 40.
12. Ibid., 9. Emphasis in the original.

Now, a feature of 'Blue buttercups abound (or are rare, or are numerous)' is that the predicates obviously attribute no property at all to any blue buttercup. It is even more obvious if we consider the invalidity of inferring from that proposition the nonsensical conclusion that some individual buttercup b abounds (or is rare or is numerous). And, if 'exists' invariably belongs to the same family as 'some,' 'abounds,' 'rare,' and 'numerous,' it would make no more sense to infer from 'Blue buttercups exist' that an individual buttercup b exists than it would to infer from 'Blue buttercups abound' that b abounds. In all these cases 'blue buttercups' is to be taken to refer not to *individual* buttercups, but to a *property*, namely, the property of being a blue buttercup. And what is being said is simply that this property is instantiated in numerous individuals ('Blue buttercups are numerous'), or merely in some individuals ('Blue buttercups exist'). Thus, 'Blue buttercups do not exist' is saying merely that the property of being a blue buttercup is not instantiated in anything.

The conclusion about the logical structure of general existential propositions is obviously of a piece with the view that has been current since Frege, and which would exhibit the logical structure of 'Some buttercups are blue' more perspicuously as 'For some x (x is a buttercup and x is blue),' i.e., '$(\exists x)(x$ is a buttercup & x is blue).' The significance of this is its recognition that 'buttercups' is not being used as a (common) name but as a predicable, namely, 'is a buttercup.' Predicables, however, refer not to individuals but to properties. Now the paradox associated with 'Blue buttercups do not exist' could arise only if 'blue buttercups' were taken to refer to individual blue buttercups. Since it refers only to a property—the property of being a blue buttercup—there is simply no paradox. With this treatment of the majority of *general* existential propositions I have no quarrel.[13]

Williams recognized that his treatment of 'exists' in general propositions would not work with singular ones, for 'Lord Hailsham

---

13. I say 'the majority' because, although the view is applicable to the general proposition 'Elephants exist, but mermaids do not,' I have argued elsewhere that it is not applicable to the equally general 'Elephants exist, but dinosaurs do not.' Cf. 'In Defence of the Predicate "Exists,"' *Mind* 84 (1975): 338–54.

is numerous' and 'Lord Hailsham is not none' make no sense at all. He recognized, too, that there has surely to be some escape from the paradox that he took to arise if 'exists' were a first-level predicate. Hence his Frege-like suggestion that 'Lord Hailsham exists' says nothing at all about Lord Hailsham himself but merely about the name 'Lord Hailsham,' namely, that it has been used to designate a real individual rather than a fictional one: the proposition is about a name, not a person.[14] On this understanding, the paradox that was based on the supposition that the propositions were about individuals would simply not arise.

Geach, however, has countered the suggestion that 'Lord Hailsham exists' is merely about the name 'Lord Hailsham' by offering biblical examples in which this is clearly false.[15] One such is Jacob's bewailing the loss of his sons in 'Joseph is not and Simeon is not.'[16] He makes the reasonable comment that 'it would be quite absurd to say that Jacob in uttering those words was not talking about Joseph and Simeon but about the use of their names.'[17] Similar examples are the report of God saying to Moses 'I am who am'[18] (i.e., 'I am he who *is*) and Christ's claim 'Before Abraham was, I am.' [19]

Williams, however, interprets Jacob's cry as elliptical for 'Joseph no longer is and Simeon no longer is.'[20] He then treats these propositions as embedding both 'Joseph is' and 'Simeon is,' and deals with them in a way to which I shall return shortly. As for the others, he suggests that the biblical authors were no less mistaken in their understanding of their own language than they were about the origins

---

14. C. J. F. Williams, *Being, Identity, and Truth,* 34.

15. P. T. Geach, 'Form and Existence,' *Proceedings of the Aristotelian Society* 55 (1954–55), reprinted in his *God and the Soul* (London: Routledge and Kegan Paul, 1969), 42–64.

16. Genesis 42:36. King James version.

17. P. T. Geach, *God and the Soul,* 58.

18. Exodus 3:14. King James version.

19. John 8:58. King James version. Recall from earlier in the chapter that the value of this and the earlier example lies not in their accuracy as translations, but in the quality of the English in which the translations are expressed.

20. C. J. F. Williams, *What Is Existence?* 146.

of the universe. He argues that, 'if God's revelation can be made in words which presuppose historical misconceptions [about the origin of the universe], it can presumably be made through words whose correct use has equally been misconceived.'[21] Well, hardly. It really is drawing the longbow exceeding taut to equate the biblical authors' knowledge of their own language with their ignorance of competing versions of the Big Bang theory, and to imply that they were no less likely to be ignorant of the former than they were of the latter. No one could expect them to know anything about the Big Bang theory, nor even about philosophical logic. It defies credulity, however, to suggest that they were equally ignorant of so rudimentary a difference as that between saying something about the individuals Simeon and Joseph and saying something about their names. Had they been so afflicted they could hardly have written the Old Testament.

In leaving this dispute unresolved for the moment, it is worth noting that even someone sympathetic to the view that stand-alone uses of 'Lord Hailsham exists' are not about Lord Hailsham might well hesitate to say the same about the so-called embedded occurrences of that proposition. I refer to those that occur in propositions like 'Lord Hailsham no longer exists' and 'Lord Hailsham might never have existed,' to mention but a couple. The former might be understood as 'It is no longer the case that (Lord Hailsham exists)' and the latter as 'It might never have been the case that (Lord Hailsham exists)'; and, as thus understood, 'Lord Hailsham exists' would seem to be a genuine logical component of both propositions. What also seems quite clear, however, is that the propositions as a whole are about Lord Hailsham: neither of them is about his name. But surely their being about Lord Hailsham can stem only from the presence of 'Lord Hailsham exists' within them. Here, then, are some apparently incontestable examples of 'Lord Hailsham exists' being about a person rather than a name.

Williams agrees: he concedes that 'Lord Hailsham no longer exists' and 'Lord Hailsham might never have existed' are 'propositions which genuinely say something about a real man': they are 'not propo-

---

21. C. J. F. Williams, *Being, Identity, and Truth*, 36.

sitions about names nor are the properties they ascribe properties of classes or concepts.'[22] What he denies, however, is that the something said of Lord Hailsham is 'exists'; for to say otherwise would, he thinks, be tantamount to embracing the very paradox he has been striving to avoid. To justify his denial he has therefore to reconcile the following two claims:

- 'Lord Hailsham no longer exists' and 'Lord Hailsham might never have existed' are admittedly about Lord Hailsham. At first sight, what they predicate of him would seem to be 'exists.'
- It is impossible, under pain of paradox, that 'Lord Hailsham no longer exists' and 'Lord Hailsham might never have existed' predicate 'exists' of Lord Hailsham, since there would be no Lord Hailsham for it to be predicated of.

Obviously, all will be well if the apparent first-level use of 'exists' can be eliminated: there will then be no paradox. Williams therefore moves to dispense with the first-level existential predicate and replace it with a *non*-existential one.[23] The strategy in regard to 'Lord Hailsham no longer exists' is to remind us that 'when we are attempting to discover whether something is the same as something which possessed some property at an earlier time, we need predicables of reidentification.' As he explains, this means that we need two predicables, one being true of Lord Hailsham before he died and the other true of him after his death. Hence his claim that 'Lord Hailsham no longer exists' is to be understood simply as the denial that there is any such pair of predicables. The proposition has therefore to be understood as 'There is no pair of predicables of reidentification such that one of them can be truly predicated of Lord Hailsham and the other truly predicated of someone at the present moment.'[24] Notice that this still contains an existential predicate, albeit not a first-level one but merely the second-level one 'there is.'

---

22. Ibid., 28.
23. Ibid., 28–33.
24. Ibid., 33.

The virtue of this interpretation, says Williams, is that it says something without, however, implying either that there is nothing for it to be about or that there is a fact of which a nonexistent Lord Hailsham would have to be a constituent. Hence, although 'Lord Hailsham no longer exists' would be nonsense if 'exists' were to be used in a first-level sense, it would make perfectly good sense if a second-level sense were employed in the proposed reparsing.

A similar strategy is followed with 'Lord Hailsham might never have existed.' Williams begins by denying that this can be understood as 'It might have been the case that it was not always the case that (Lord Hailsham exists).' He maintains, rather, that the 'not' has to occur within the brackets, as in 'It might have been the case that it was always the case that (Lord Hailsham does not exist).' As in the earlier case, this move, too, relies precariously on denying any distinction between internal and external negation. By allowing only internal negation, Williams feels able to charge the proposition with attempting not only to say something about a person but to imply that there is no such person to say anything about. It would be an attempt to present a fact about Lord Hailsham without his being a constituent of that fact.

As in the case of 'Lord Hailsham no longer exists,' the problem with 'Lord Hailsham might never have existed' is to find an interpretation in which 'exists' would not even seem to be predicated of Lord Hailsham. The suggested candidate is, 'There is a property which was an essential property of Lord Hailsham, and it might have been the case that nothing at all ever possessed this property.'[25] Obviously, this does not imply that there is any fact having a nonexistent Lord Hailsham as one of its constituents. Consequently, propositions like 'Lord Hailsham might never have existed' are said to be acceptable, but only if they are understood as being about one of Lord Hailsham's properties rather than about Lord Hailsham himself. In that case 'exists' would occur merely as a second-level predicate, which is innocuous, rather than as a first-level level one, which is not.

---

25. Ibid., 30. An example of what he means by an essential property is *being a daughter of Rosa and Manoah Bottrill,* which is attributable to his mother. About it he notes that 'there may be other things which are in this way essential to my mother's existence.'

If Williams is right, the two propositions which seemed for all the world to say something about Lord Hailsham are, mirabile dictu, saying nothing at all about him, but only about the instantiation of one or other of his properties. 'Lord Hailsham might never have existed' is saying that there is an essential property which belonged to Lord Hailsham and which might have belonged to no one. 'Lord Hailsham no longer exists' is saying that there is no pair of properties of reidentification one of which belongs to someone now, the other of which did belong to Lord Hailsham during his lifetime.

To sum up. Williams makes basically the same point about general and singular existential propositions alike. It is, first, that the negative ones do seem to generate a paradox and, second, that the appearance of paradox stems from the misconception that 'exists' functions as a first-level predicate. The challenge for him, therefore, has been to show that it need never be used as a first-level predicate at all. In attempting to meet that challenge, he argues that 'exists' is in fact being used in the following ways:

- In *general* existential propositions like 'Blue buttercups do not exist' the use of 'exists' is as a second-level predicate, which entails that the propositions are not about individuals at all, but only about properties or kinds.
- In *free-standing singular* existential propositions like 'Lord Hailsham exists' there can be no first-level use of 'exists' since 'Lord Hailsham' does not refer to any individual, but merely to itself— a name.
- In *embedded singular* existential propositions 'Lord Hailsham' does indeed refer to an individual, but 'exists' is not predicated of him. On the contrary, 'exists' is in effect merely a filler for one or other *non*-existential predicate.

Response to the Arguments from Paradox and Absurdity

Williams' views on *singular* existential propositions have been driven by two convictions, one being that they do seem to generate both paradox and absurdity, and the other that the paradox cannot be removed by treating 'exists' as a second-level predicate, as had been done successfully for general propositions. Few would deny the latter point. As to the former, the paradox and absurdity need to be treated separately. The putative *paradox,* it will be recalled, is the claim that any singular negative existential proposition like 'Lord Hailsham does not exist' can be true only if there is, paradoxically, a Lord Hailsham for it to be true of, i.e., only if he *does* exist. Or, as formulated otherwise, the paradox is that the truth of 'Lord Hailsham does not exist' would imply that there was a fact with a nonexistent as a constituent.

The so-called paradox, however, is illusory, for it arises purely from confusing a name's reference with its bearer. In particular, proponents of the paradox are confusing the reference of 'Lord Hailsham' with its bearer, as Geach, quoting Wittgenstein, once remarked.[26] The truth of 'Lord Hailsham does not exist' requires only that 'Lord Hailsham' have a reference. To have a reference, however, does not require that the bearer exist *now,* but merely that it does exist *or has existed.* Once that is recognized, there is nothing even odd, let alone paradoxical, about propositions like 'Lord Hailsham does not exist.'

The so-called *absurdity* to which Williams alludes stems not from allowing existence to be a property but from allowing *non-*existence to be one. Only if nonexistence were some kind of real property would any sheep-farmer be led to the absurdity of inspecting his flock 'with the aim of sorting the existing sheep from the nonexistent ones.' Similarly in regard to the horticulturalist examining several specimens of blue buttercup before concluding that none of them exist. And similarly with regard to Lord Hailsham, for only if nonexistence were a real property would it seem paradoxical that 'does not exist' could be true of him after there was any Lord Hailsham for it to be true of. Only if nonexistence were a real property rather than a Cambridge one could 'Lord Hailsham no longer exists' imply that Lord Hailsham had suffered some posthumous loss. If we are mindful of this, therefore, it might seem strange to lay the blame on treating

---

26. P. T. Geach, *God and the Soul,* 58–59. G. E. L. Owen makes precisely the same point in 'Aristotle and the Snares of Ontology,' in R. Bambrough, ed., *New Essays on Plato and Aristotle* (London: Routledge and Kegan Paul, 1965), 69–96.

existence as a real property of individuals, when it should surely have been laid on treating nonexistence as one. Why deny that existence is a real property, when it was necessary only to deny that nonexistence was one?

Perhaps the answer lies in the mistaken belief that the two denials are inseparable, so that there could be no denying reality to nonexistence as a property of individuals without denying it to existence also. After all, if properties are what predicates stand for, how could it be said that 'exists' stood for a real property, but that 'does not exist' did not? If we accept existence as a real property, are we not bound also to accept nonexistence as one? Clearly, these suggestions rest on two assumptions that need now to be tested, namely:

- that 'Lord Hailsham does not exist' contains a negative existential predicate.
- that a negative existential predicate stands for a real property.

In regard to the first, although 'does not exist' is a grammatical predicate in 'Lord Hailsham does not exist,' it does not follow that it must also be a logical one. We need to recognize the possibility of construing the proposition as having the logical form of 'It is not the case that (Lord Hailsham exists).' In that case, what is *predicated* of Lord Hailsham would be simply 'exists,' though this would not be *asserted* of him. What would be asserted is that it is not the case that Lord Hailsham exists. On such an analysis of singular negative existential propositions, 'does not exist' need not be recognized as a logical predicate at all, and hence would not refer to anything at all, let alone to nonexistence. Thus, there would be no grounds for the alleged absurdity.

The distinction being invoked above is one between internal or predicate negation on the one hand and external or propositional negation on the other. The difference between them has sometimes been thought to be that 'Lord Hailsham (does not exist)' says something about the individual Lord Hailsham, whereas 'It is not the case that (Lord Hailsham exists)' says something about a proposition, namely, that the proposition 'Lord Hailsham does not exist' is false. On the contrary, nothing is said about a proposition in either case. Rather, in both cases something is said about an individual, namely,

Lord Hailsham; the cases differ only in *what* they say about him. The former purports to say that nonexistence is had by Lord Hailsham, to which Williams rightly objects. The latter says that it is not the case that existence is had by Lord Hailsham, and that is quite unobjectionable.

Williams has dismissed the distinction between internal and external negation as 'a distinction without a difference.' Admittedly, there is no place for it in predicate logic, but that consideration could be decisive only if predicate logic were as all-embracing as natural language, which it patently is not. To put the issue beyond doubt, however, consider the example of 'a is not moral' which may mean either of two things. It may mean that *a* has the property of being non-moral; alternatively, it may simply be denying that *a* has the property of being moral. Internal negation ('*a* (is not moral)') is being used in the first case, external negation ('It is not the case that (*a* is moral)') in the second. If, then, the distinction between internal and external negation were one without a difference, those two renderings should always be interchangeable. Yet, that is clearly false; for the first is to be taken as '*a* is immoral,' but the second as the quite different '*a* is either immoral or amoral.' Contrary to Williams, therefore, the distinction is a substantive one, and presents a major threat to his case against a first-level use of 'exists.'

That being so, it is certainly not a matter of indifference whether 'Lord Hailsham does not exist' is rendered as '(Lord Hailsham) does not exist' or as 'It is not the case that (Lord Hailsham exists).' Because it is the former but not the latter that gives rise to problems, the latter is clearly to be chosen. In that case, 'does not exist' would not occur as a *logical* predicate in 'Lord Hailsham does not exist'; and so we could recognize existence as a real property without the embarrassment of having also to recognize nonexistence as real. One might have thought that even those who admit only external negation (and deny any difference between it and internal negation) would be able to accept this conclusion.

There is, nevertheless, a further objection that might now be raised, for even if 'does not exist' has no logical role in 'Lord Hailsham does not exist,' it must surely be admitted that 'It is not the case that ___ exists' does have such a role, and that it is indeed a negative predicate. Since it is a negative predicate, and since properties are what predicates stand for, are we not irretrievably committed to the occurrence of some negative existential property? If so, there will have been no escape from the 'absurdities' of existence after all.

Of course, it can hardly be denied that by removing the name 'Lord Hailsham' from 'It is not the case that (Lord Hailsham exists)' we obtain the negative predicate 'It is not the case that ___ exists.' However, the property for which it stands cannot be a real one. Why? Because that predicate does not occur in what Dummett would call the constructional history of 'It is not the case that (Lord Hailsham exists),' which is as follows:

- Remove the proper name from an arbitrary proposition 'Caesar exists' to form the predicable '___ exists.'
- Insert 'Lord Hailsham' in the gap in '___ exists' to form 'Lord Hailsham exists.'
- Insert that proposition in the gap in 'It is not the case that ___' to form 'It is not the case that Lord Hailsham exists.'

The point of drawing attention to the constructional history is not merely to show how the proposition is to be formed but, more importantly, to reveal its ontological commitments. Those commitments can be inferred only from the *logical* parts employed in its constructional history. Clearly, the predicable 'It is not the case that ___ exists' plays no part at all in that process. Consequently, the property to which it refers can be no more than a Cambridge one.

Absurdity, however, could arise only from nonexistence being either a real property or among such Cambridge ones (if any) whose acquisition is conditional upon their subjects of attribution existing at that time. Since nonexistence is not only a Cambridge property, but one that requires no such precondition, it fails to satisfy that condition; and hence its attribution to a deceased Lord Hailsham generates no absurdity whatever. So much for considering 'Lord Hailsham does not exist' as employing external negation.

That is not all, for absurdity can be shown not to arise even if, as Williams thinks, the negation in 'Lord Hailsham does not exist' had to be *internal*. Once again, a predicable can be obtained by removing 'Lord Hailsham' from the proposition, though this time it will not be 'it is not the case that ___ exists,' but simply '___ does not exist.' The question is whether that predicable stands for a real rather than a Cambridge property; and, once again, the first point to determine is whether it forms part of the proposition's constructional history, which is as follows:

- Remove the proper name from an arbitrary proposition, 'Caesar exists,' to obtain the predicable '___ exists.'
- Negate this predicable to form '___ does not exist.'
- Insert 'Lord Hailsham' in the gap in '___ does not exist' to form '(Lord Hailsham)(does not exist).'

Since 'does not exist' *does* form part of this constructional history, we are as yet not entitled to preclude its referent from being a real property. We therefore need some criterion for determining whether nonexistence is a Cambridge property even though existence is a real one. In general terms, we need some criterion for determining when F's being a real property would entail that non-F is also a real property. For the moment, let us consider this not in regard to existence but in regard to the property red. The issue is whether the absence of redness from something which could be red (a real property) must bespeak the presence of a correlative property which, too, is real. Certainly, if b were a piece of wood then it could lack redness only if it had some hue other than red—be it brown, cream, fawn, or whatever—none of which could be dismissed as mere Cambridge properties. That does not settle the question, however, since the result would be very different if b were not a piece of wood but a piece of glass. Now, although glass is like wood in being something that *could* be red, it is also unlike wood in that its failure to be red does not mean that it has any color at all: it may be quite colorless.

To say that the glass is nonred is therefore not to say that it has any *correlative* property, or at least not any that is real. It might of course be said to have the property of being noncolored; but, then, so too might a pain or a flash of insight, though their being noncolored could hardly be claimed as a real, rather than a Cambridge, property. Reflecting on this example, it is not difficult to see that lack of a real property F would bespeak the presence of a correlative *real* property non-F only if F and non-F were determinates of the one determinable property. [27] Thus, if red and non-red were related as determinates of the one determinable (color), red could be absent from an individual b only if some other determinate of *color* were present in b.

The relevance to the discussion of nonexistence is fairly clear. If lack of existence in b (which had existed) were to bespeak the presence in b of nonexistence as a real rather than as a Cambridge property, existence and nonexistence should be related to some real property just as red and non-red are related to the real determinable which is color. Then, just as red and non-red would both have had to be understood as determinates of a common determinable (color), so existence and nonexistence would have both to be understood as determinates of the determinable—if any—that is common to them both. There is, however, no determinable common to them both. Consequently, ascribing lack of existence to b (which had existed) does not bespeak the presence in b of nonexistence as a real property rather than a Cambridge one.

Hence, even if the predicate in 'Lord Hailsham does not exist' truly were 'does not exist,' the property to which it referred could be no more than a Cambridge one. No absurdity could arise, therefore, from allowing 'does not exist' to be a first-level predicate in 'Lord Hailsham does not exist.' This had already been demonstrated in the case of negation being external to the proposition; it has now been demonstrated for internal negation as well. No matter whether Williams is right or wrong about the lack of distinction between internal and external negation, the result is the same: no absurdity arises from singular negative existential propositions.

---

27. The determinable/determinate distinction differs from the species/genus one. In the latter case one could say, for example, 'Socrates is an animal that is rational,' thereby specifying how Socrates differs from a kangaroo. Nothing comparable can be said in the former case, for one cannot *specify* just what the difference is between color and red. See A. N. Prior, 'Determinables, Determinates, and Determinants,' *Mind* 58 (1949): 1–20 and 178–94; J. Searle and S. Körner, 'Determinables and the Notion of Resemblance,' *Proceedings of the Aristotelian Society,* supp. vol. (1958): 125–58.

In this section, then, I have been arguing that there are no acceptable grounds for the widespread belief which denies that 'Lord Hailsham no longer exists' contains 'exists' as a first-level predicate. The belief rests on the assumption that, if 'exists' really were a first-level predicate, there could be no denying that 'Lord Hailsham no longer exists' contains a negative existential predicate, namely, either 'does not exist' or 'it is no longer the case that ___ exists.' In either case, so it is claimed, there would be no escaping the absurdity of regarding nonexistence as a real property. Such an argument employs the following three main premises, the first two of which are quite explicit, but the third merely implicit:

- Predicables are formed by removing a proper name from a proposition.
- Predicables stand for properties.
- Any negative existential property would have either to be a *real* one, or, if a Cambridge property, it must be one whose acquisition is conditional upon its subject of attribution existing at that time.

I accept the first; and I accept the second as well. What I do not accept is the third. As I have argued, the third is not true of the property referred to by the predicable 'it is not the case that ___ exists.' The same point holds even if the negation is taken to be internal, and the predicate is 'does not exist.' There, too, the relevant property is a Cambridge one. Thus, *no matter whether the distinction between internal and external negation in this context is accepted or rejected,* the result is the same. In neither case are we committed to Lord Hailsham acquiring any property, real or Cambridge, whose acquisition is conditional upon his existing at that time. In neither case, therefore, does 'Lord Hailsham does not exist' generate the alleged absurdities which would debar 'exists' from being a first-level predicate. There is indeed no such bar.

An Overview

Williams proposed a tripartite solution to the putative paradox of negative existential propositions—one for general propositions like 'Blue buttercups exist,' one for stand-alone occurrences of propositions like 'Lord Hailsham exists,' and another for embedded occurrences as in propositions like 'Lord Hailsham no longer exists' and 'Lord Hailsham might never have existed.'

So far as *general* propositions are concerned, his Fregean analysis treats common nouns not as names at all but merely as predicables. This means that, in such propositions, 'exists' will not function as a first-level predicate but as a second-level one. It means also that the propositions will be about properties rather than individuals. And, for both these reasons, it means that the alleged paradox simply does not arise—if the propositions are general.[28]

In regard to singular propositions like 'Lord Hailsham does not exist,' the paradox was illusory, since it was based on the misguided assumption that 'Lord Hailsham' must have a *bearer,* whereas all it needs is a *reference.* Although there can be no reference to anything that has *never* existed, there can indeed be reference to what *no longer* exists: the reference does not die with the bearer. In regard to the two propositions in which 'Lord Hailsham exists' were embedded, absurdity arose only on the assumption that nonexistence was a real property, rather than the Cambridge one that it so patently is.

At the conclusion of this section, therefore, there are no grounds for thinking that either paradox or absurdity is generated by recognizing 'exists' as predicable of individuals. Nor, therefore, is there any reason for accepting the strained reparsings of 'Lord Hailsham no longer exists' and 'Lord Hailsham might never have existed' which Williams was driven to propose. Each of those propositions is quite straightforwardly about Lord Hailsham, and not about one or other of his properties. That, however, is not the end of the story, for there are further objections which need to be rebutted before concluding that 'exists' can in fact be used as a first-level predicate.

---

28. Recall that the accusation of *paradox* is that if 'exists' were predicable of concrete individuals, then propositions like 'Socrates does not exist' could be true only if there were no Socrates for it to be true of. The accusation of *absurdity* is that existence could be a real property of individuals only if nonexistence were also a real property of them.

II. Further Objections to 'Exists' Being Predicable of Individuals

Obviously, there would be no role for a first-level use of 'exists' if there were no proper names to which they could be attached to form a singular proposition. It is to that point that Russell and Quine appeal in denying that 'exists' is ever a first-level predicate. For their different reasons each argues that, because proper names are superfluous, 'exists' is not predicable of individuals.

Russell on 'Socrates exists'
As noted in the preceding chapter, Russellian-type views on existence could be summed up as claiming:

- 'Exists' is always a second-level predicate, never a first-level one.
- Existence is always a property of propositional functions, never a property of individuals.

There is nothing controversial about Russell's treatment of general existential propositions like 'Dragons exist,' which he would reparse as 'The propositional function "is a dragon" is satisfied at least once,' i.e. '$(\exists x)(x$ is a dragon).' Not so uncontroversial, however, is his treating singular existential propositions like 'Socrates exists' in essentially the same way. In accordance with his views on proper names as really disguised descriptions, 'Socrates exists' would be transformed into some such proposition as 'The teacher of Plato exists,' a form of proposition to which his theory of descriptions would then be applicable. It could thus be transformed into 'Exactly one thing is a teacher of Plato' or 'The propositional function "___ is a teacher of Plato" is satisfied exactly once,' i.e. '$(\exists x)[Fx \,\&\, (y)(Fy \supset x = y)]$,' where '$Fx$' does duty for '$x$ is a teacher of Plato.' In this way all singular existential propositions would be assimilated to general ones, and every occurrence of 'exists' would be a second-level one. Furthermore, the property of existence would generate no problems, since it would now be a property not of individuals but merely of propositional functions. Indeed, in regard to actual things in the world, he concludes that 'it is a sheer mistake to say there is anything analogous to existence that you can say about them.'

Although ingenious, Russell's approach fails as an account of singular existential propositions, for Kripke has shown that, as rigid designators, proper names cannot be reduced to definite descriptions. A further objection, however, is that Russell's approach fails to distinguish between two kinds of uniqueness. One is the uniqueness of a *precise* individual which, while achieved by *non*-fictional proper names, is unattainable by descriptions or predicates of any kind. The other kind is the uniqueness of *precisely one* individual, which is the most that predicates and descriptions can achieve.

Let me enlarge on this briefly with the help of the following two propositions:

2.1   The one and only individual that is *F* is thinking dark thoughts.

2.2   Socrates is thinking dark thoughts.

In regard to 2.2 it would make sense to point to an individual and ask, 'Is *that* the individual that 2.2 is about?' for the proposition can be made true only by the particular individual that is Socrates. There is, on the contrary, no such particular individual required to make 2.1 true. It would be true if there were *any* (though, admittedly, only one) individual that is *F*. For that reason, although it would make sense to point to an individual that is *F* and ask 'Is 2.1 *satisfied* by that individual?' it would make no sense whatever to ask 'Is that the individual that 2.1 is *about*?' The individual pointed to may make 2.1 true, but it cannot be the one that 2.1 is about, since *any* individual that is *F* would make 2.1 true, provided it were the only individual to be *F*. Precisely one individual is required to make 2.1 true, but no precise one.

The distinction I am drawing would be of dubious value if, as Strawson once claimed, the notion of what a proposition is *about* were far from clear. However, the notion could hardly be clearer: what a proposition is about is determined by the kind of logical analysis (or analyses) to which it is amenable. The general rule to be followed is that what a proposition is about is whatever its logical part of lowest level stands for. This rule applies no matter what the analysis of the proposition may be, and even when there is more than one acceptable analysis of it. For example, 'Socrates is thinking dark thoughts' can be analyzed as composed of a name ('Socrates') and a first-level predicate ('___ is thinking dark thoughts'). The proposition is *about* whatever the expression of lower-level ('Socrates') stands for, namely, Socrates. The higher-level expression tells us just what is being said about Socrates, namely, that he is thinking dark thoughts.

Of course, the very same proposition admits also of a different analysis, namely, '(Of Socrates it is true that)(he is thinking dark thoughts),' in which case it is taken to be composed of the first-level predicable '___ is thinking dark thoughts' and the second-level predicate ('of Socrates it is true that)(he ___).' As so analyzed, it would be about the thinking of dark thoughts: and what was being said about it would be that the thinking of dark thoughts occurs in Socrates. Exactly the same kind of analysis applies to 'The one and only individual that is F is thinking dark thoughts,' for it is composed of the first-level predicable '___ is F & ___ is thinking dark thoughts' and the second-level predicate 'Exactly one thing is such that (it. . . . it ___).' Thus, what the proposition is about is the conjunction of being F and of thinking dark thoughts; and what is being said about that conjunction is that it has exactly one instance. While this proposition admits of a first-level/second-level analysis, it nevertheless differs from 'Socrates is thinking dark thoughts' in *not* admitting of a name/first-level one.

There is thus a quite clear distinction between what each of 2.1 and 2.2 are about. Proposition 2.2 admits of a name/first-level analysis as well as a first-level/second-level one, and hence can be said to be either about Socrates or about the thinking of dark thoughts, depending on which analysis is employed. As we have seen, however, proposition 2.1 can be said to be about the thinking of dark thoughts, but not about Socrates.[29] Thus, 2.1 cannot be an adequate rendering of 2.2 for, although both may be made true by Socrates, only 2.2 can be *about* Socrates.

---

29. Of course, the *speaker* may be thinking about Socrates while uttering 2.1 or may even intend it to be understood that it is Socrates who is thinking the dark thoughts. The point I am making, however, concerns neither what the speaker may have in mind or may intend, but what the proposition is about.

Precisely the same point can be made about the suggestion that 'Socrates exists' should be understood as 'Exactly one thing is a teacher of Plato, etc.' The point is that while 'Socrates exists' can be taken to be about Socrates, its proposed substitute cannot be so taken, and hence fails as an adequate reparsing of 'Socrates exists.'

Quine on 'Socrates exists'
Writing about the proposition 'Pegasus exists,' Quine once suggested:

> If the notion of Pegasus had been so obscure or so basic a one that no pat translation into a descriptive phrase had offered itself along familiar lines, we could still have availed ourselves of the following artificial and trivial-seeming device: we could have appealed to the *ex hypothesi* unanalysable, irreducible attribute of *being Pegasus* adopting, for its expression, the verb 'is-Pegasus,' or 'pegasizes.'[30]

Thus, 'Pegasus exists' would become 'Something pegasizes,' i.e., '$(\exists x)(x$ pegasizes).' Likewise, 'Socrates exists' would become 'Something socratizes,' i.e., '$(\exists x)(x$ socratizes).'[31]

It might be argued that this proposal cannot be charged with not being about Socrates, for 'Socrates' does occur in '$(\exists x)(x =$ Socrates),' which can therefore be viewed quite properly as composed of the name 'Socrates' and the first-level predicate '$(\exists x)(x = \_\_\_),$' i.e., 'Something is identical with ___.' Now, although it could well be viewed in that way, that seems not to have been Quine's intention, for his express aim was to eliminate proper names in deference to predicates: the name 'Socrates' was to be eliminated in deference to the predicate 'socratizes.' Assuming that such a predicate really does eliminate 'Socrates' rather than merely provide a shorthand for '= Socrates,' then, unlike 'Socrates exists,' '$(\exists x)(x$ socratizes)' would not be *about* Socrates at all even though it would of course be made

30. W. V. Quine, 'On What There Is,' in his *From a Logical Point of View* (New York: Harper, 1963), 7–8. Emphasis in the original.

31. W. V. Quine, *Word and Object* (Cambridge: MIT Press, 1960), 179.

true or false by him. And that means that, while 'Socrates exists' is about Socrates, Quine's reparsing of it would not be. It thus fails for the same reason as did Russell's.

Dummett on 'Socrates exists'

Michael Dummett seems to have three objections to 'exists' being predicable of Socrates. The first is that, 'even if there are two distinguishable uses of "exists," these senses are evidently connected' which, in his view, is impossible. Why? Because, as he rightly says, they are of *different logical types,* one a first-level predicate and the other a second-level one. Because no 'difference of sense could be greater than one between a quantifier and a first-level predicate,' he concludes that the two uses of 'the verb "exists" would be simply equivocal.'[32] Consequently, there can be no room for *both* a first- and a second-level use of 'exists.' Which, then, is to be discarded? Since the second-level use is beyond question, the first-level use has to go.

That argument, however, is altogether too swift. Although no one would wish to question the absolute divide between different logical types, that does not license the conclusion that the two uses of 'exists' are equivocal. Rather, all that can be concluded is that they are *either* equivocal *or* analogical—either casually ambiguous[33] or systematically ambiguous. Without examining particular cases, it would be difficult to determine just which conclusion was the correct one.

Fortunately, a particular case has in fact been provided by Geach.[34] Consider the two propositions 'Hiawatha is disappearing' said as Hiawatha disappears into the distance, and 'The American Indians are disappearing.' In the former, 'disappearing' is predicated of an individual; in the latter, it is being said not of individuals but of a race, a species. Here, therefore, are two logically different uses of 'disappearing,' a first- and a second-level use. Yet, although there is

---

32. M. Dummett, *Frege, Philosophy of Language,* 2nd ed. (London: Duckworth, 1981), 386.

33. Examples of casual ambiguity are 'bank' as in 'river bank' and 'commercial bank' or 'rare' as in 'rare steak' and 'rare species.'

34. Mentioned in C. J. F. Williams, *What Is Existence?* 71.

no univocity between the two senses, they are not totally unconnected, as they should be if Dummett's argument were to succeed. The mere fact of their being different logical types is thus no evidence of their being equivocal. Nor therefore does it preclude any first-level use of 'exists.'

For those who have difficulty in detecting any similarity between the two senses of 'disappearing' in Geach's example let me suggest a development of it. Consider Tasmanian tigers and the last of them that died in captivity some decades ago. I shall call him 'Tim.' Suppose, anachronistically, that Tim had been hit by a ray gun and disappeared without trace in a blinding flash. Of course, at that very moment his species, too, would have disappeared from the face of the earth. The former use of 'disappeared' is a first-level one, and the latter a second-level one. Call them 'disappeared$_1$' and 'disappeared$_2$' respectively.

Now, two things can be said about those uses:

- They are not univocal.
- Neither are they *totally* dissimilar, because 'disappearance$_2$ of the species' entails 'disappearance$_1$ of each its members,' and 'disappearance$_1$ of the last member' entails 'disappearance$_2$ of the species.'

It is characteristic of analogical expressions that their senses are neither univocal nor totally dissimilar (as distinct from being purely equivocal). This is exactly the case with 'disappeared$_1$' and 'disappeared$_2$' and, I suggest, with 'exists$_1$' and 'exists$_2$' as well.[35]

In his second objection Dummett wants to maintain that 'Cleopatra no longer exists' cannot be taken at face value, i.e., as saying that Cleopatra *no longer* has a certain property. He reasons that it would commit us to saying that there is such a person as Cleopatra, who no longer has the property of existing. But this, he says, is just

---

35. Note that 'disappears$_1$' is not synonymous with 'ceases to exist$_1$,' for when Jack Kennedy 'ceased to exist' we did not say that he disappeared. Nor is 'disappeared$_2$' synonymous with 'exists$_2$,' for 'disappeared$_2$' means merely 'ceases to be instantiated,' not 'ceases to exist$_2$'.

as absurd as saying there is such a substance as phlogiston, which lacks the timeless property of existing. Well, is it?

The absurdity in the phlogiston example arises from its being a case of make-believe parading as reality. On the other hand, although the language may be rather angular, there is no absurdity in 'There are such things as dinosaurs which no longer have the property of existing.' Absurdity would arise only if 'existing' were being used in the very same sense as 'there are' (the second-level sense), for in that case the proposition would be saying 'There are dinosaurs which there are not,' The fact is, however, that the proposition would be expressed more perspicuously as '$(\exists x)(x$ is a dinosaur & x does not exist)' which contains no such contradiction since 'exist' is a first-level predicate whereas '$(\exists x)(x \underline{\quad})$' is a second-level one. Similarly, the Cleopatra example would be '$(\exists x)(x$ is a person & y is named 'Cleopatra' & it is no longer the case that $(z$ exists) & $x = y = z)$'. No absurdity arises in either the dinosaur or Cleopatra cases, precisely because 'exists' is a first-level predicate but '$(\exists x)(x \underline{\quad})$' is a second-level one. The former can be said solely of individuals, whereas the latter can be said solely of properties, which in the present case are the properties of being a person and being named 'Cleopatra.' There is an unbridgeable gulf between predicates of different levels. Consequently, there can be no absurdity in conjoining negation at one level with affirmation at the other level. This is so in tenseless language no less than in a tensed one: in neither case can the difference in level be ignored.

It would appear that Dummett's objection to accepting existence (or nonexistence) as a *property* is that he can make no sense of existence being *lost* or of nonexistence being *gained*. Against this way of speaking he argues that 'beauty is a property which Cleopatra had when a woman, and may have lacked as a baby: but existence, even when temporal, is not a property that may be first acquired and later lost.'[36] Defenders of the two-sense thesis would not want to disagree. Indeed, that is precisely why they insist that propositions like 'Cleopatra no longer exists,' 'Cleopatra came to exist,' and 'Cleopatra ceased to exist' are to be understood in such a way as certainly *not* to imply either loss of existence or its acquisition. Rather, they are to

---

36. M. Dummett, *Frege, Philosophy of Language*, 387.

be understood respectively as 'It is no longer the case that (Cleopatra exists),' 'It came to be that (Cleopatra exists),' and 'It ceased to be that (Cleopatra exists),' none of which carries the unacceptable implication that Cleopatra either acquires or loses any property at all.

Finally, Dummett attempts to disqualify existence from being a property with his claim that 'only things like being beautiful *at a certain stage in one's life* are properties. Properties, thus understood, are atemporal, and thus are things of which it can make no sense to say that one acquires them or loses them.'[37] In the face of his insistence that properties are restricted to being had at a certain stage in one's life, one would want to know just what he considers a property to be. For my part, I take a property to be whatever is attributable to something by a predicate.[38] Among the items covered by this very broad umbrella are first-level properties, namely, whatever is attributable to *individuals* by a predicate. And under that much smaller umbrella one has to distinguish real properties from Cambridge ones, formal from nonformal, essential from accidental, and so on.

Even within that short list there are two kinds of property—formal (being an individual) and essential (being human)—both of which belong to an individual at *every* stage of its life, thereby failing to satisfy Dummett's criterion of 'being beautiful at a certain stage in one's life.' Obviously, Dummett's demands apply only to properties that are accidents. However, although it is true that existence would indeed be accidental, it would certainly not be an accident. It would be accidental, since an individual does not exist necessarily. It would not, however, be an accident, since an individual could neither do nor be anything without it. Consequently, it is not subject to Dummett's strictures. 'Being accidental' is not to be confused with 'being an accident.'

Taken either singly or together, therefore, Dummett's objections do nothing to weaken the case for 'exists' being predicable of individuals.

---

37. Ibid. My emphasis.

38. This does not exclude properties from worlds in which there would be no one to make any attribution of them. It requires merely that individuals provide the *basis* for such attributions—should there be anyone to make them.

Jonathan Barnes on the Redundancy of 'Exists'

Yet another redundancy proposal is one presented by Jonathan Barnes, albeit quite tentatively. [39] After critizing the views of Frege, Russell, and Quine, he explores the possibility suggested by the linguist Lyons that 'exists' be analyzed 'into a "copula", "be", plus an indefinite locative: "Dodos once existed" means "Dodos once were somewhere"; "Pegasus never existed" means "Pegasus was never anywhere".'[40] In support of this proposal Barnes makes three points:

- In many languages there are phrases that can be translated sometimes by 'exist,' sometimes by a clear locative construction.
- There are 'striking similarities' between the role of 'exists' in regard to animate and inanimate things and the role of 'take place' in regard to battles and other events. Since it is highly plausible to analyze 'take place' into a copula plus locative and temporal adverb, one might infer that a similar analysis should be applicable to 'exists.'[41]
- Things that exist are most often contrasted with what do not exist—figments of the imagination, legendary figures, illusory figures, not to mention things that once existed but have ceased to do so. Common to each of the nonexistents is that they are *not* spatial. Again, therefore, it is plausible to suggest that a characteristic of things that do exist is that they are what the contrasting figures are not, namely, spatial.[42]

From these considerations Barnes concludes that 'the primary sense of "exists" may perhaps be "to be somewhere".' Qualifying this conclusion, he adds that '"exist" is not always used to mean "be

---

39. J. Barnes, *The Ontological Argument* (London: St. Martin's Press, 1972), chap. 3.

40. Ibid., 63.

41. The underlying suggestion here is that, because the single term 'place' is a spatial one, any phrase formed by adding 'take' to it should retain that spatial character. Not so, for, although both 'on' and 'over' are spatial terms, neither 'take on' nor 'take over' retain any spatial character whatever.

42. As Peter Forrest has reminded me, however, this contrast is quite unreliable, for even some *fictional* entities have spatial connotations. Thus,

somewhere" even if that constitutes its central sense. . . . "some-where" is not always used literally of spatial position, and the lin-guist's term "locative" does not refer solely to spatial location.'[43]

Neither singly nor collectively do these considerations form any-thing like a compelling case, as Barnes' use of 'perhaps' seems im-plicitly to concede. The best that might be said is that the case is highly speculative, and nowhere more so than in regard to the use of 'exists' as a predicate of concrete individuals, for these ought not be regarded as exclusively material individuals. All material entities are individual, but not all concrete individuals need be material. The mark of a concrete individual is simply that it can bring about change and/or undergo change, something that could be true of an imma-terial entity no less than of a material one. Although material indi-viduals are spatial, concrete immaterial ones are not. Hence, even if it were at all plausible that 'exists' as predicated of material indi-viduals should be rendered as 'is somewhere,' it would be decidedly implausible to say the same of 'exists' predicated of concrete imma-terial individuals, for it makes no sense to speak of their occupying any space at all. Indeed, the existence of concrete immaterial indi-viduals with intellective and volitional powers would not presuppose that there was any space whatever. Not much, therefore, can be said for the attempt to reduce 'exists' to 'is somewhere.'

'Exists' as Redundant: A Formal Predicate?

It is worth considering whether existence might not be what Wittgen-stein called a formal concept, and whether 'exists' might not be the kind of predicate that expresses such a concept, even if only im-properly. Examples of such predicates are in '2 is a number,' '"2" is a numeral,' 'Tom is an object,' '"Tom" is a name,' '"The mother of Socrates" is a complex.'

What interests us about such predicates is that, although they are undoubtedly first-level ones, they attribute no real property to what they are said of, but simply place them in some category. The propo-sitions in which they occur are like tautologies, except that their denial is not self-contradictory. 'Black stones are not black' is self-

---

Sherlock Holmes was said to live in a real street (Baker Street) and Pegasus was said to fly around a real country (Greece).

43. J. Barnes, *Ontological Argument*, 64–65.

contradictory, whereas '2 is not a number' is not, even though it can never be true. These characteristics might suggest that 'exists,' too, is a formal predicate, for it is commonly claimed that 'Socrates exists' is uninformative and that 'Socrates does not exist' is not self-contradictory, although in certain circumstances it would be extremely odd to affirm it.

An interesting feature of the propositions listed above is that, despite not being tautologies, none of them can cease to be true. 2 cannot cease being a number, '2' cannot cease being a numeral, 'Tom is an object' cannot cease being true, nor can 'Tom' cease being a proper name, though it may well fall into disuse. It may not have been necessary that there be a 2, '2,' Tom, or 'Tom'; but, given that we do have them, it can never be false to predicate the relevant formal predicates of them. It is no more true to say 'Socrates is no longer an individual' than to say '2 is no longer a number.'

It is just that characteristic of formal predicates which disqualifies 'exists' from being one of them. If 'is F' is a formal predicate, then, once 'Socrates is F' is true, it remains true even today. On the contrary, although 'Socrates exists' was once true, it is indeed now false. Hence, 'exists' cannot be a formal predicate, attractive as it may have been to think otherwise.

'Exists' as Dispensable?
An Excluder? To have ruled out 'exists' from being a formal predicate is not necessarily to have ruled out all possibility of its being a first-level predicate without existence being a real property. One other possibility is that it be what Roland Hall has called 'an excluder,'[44] and which he introduces as follows:

> Adjectives that . . . (1) are attributive as opposed to predicative, (2) serve to rule out something without themselves adding anything, and (3) ambiguously rule out different things according to context, I call 'excluders.'

As examples, he suggests 'ordinary,' 'absolute,' 'accidental,' 'barbarian,' 'base,' 'civil,' 'real,' amongst many others. The one most relevant to the present discussion, however, is 'real.'

---

44. R. Hall, 'Excluders,' *Analysis* 20 (1959–60): 1–7.

According to Hall, 'real' is the kind of adjective that merely rules out something without itself adding anything. According to context, it can rule out b's being imaginary, or artificial, or counterfeit. In doing so, however, it attributes nothing positive to what it is said of: its contribution is purely negative. Moreover, what it excludes varies with context, and therein, says Hall, lies its ambiguity. Although Hall himself does not suggest that 'exists' is an excluder, others might be tempted to do so, or even to suggest that 'exists' means nothing else but 'is real.' On either suggestion existence would not be a real property, and that is why these views might commend themselves to anyone who was bothered by the apparent difficulty in allowing existence to be a property of concrete individuals.

Let us therefore consider whether 'exists' really does have the three marks required of an excluder. Since it is not an adjective at all, it obviously cannot be an attributive one. However, that is of no account, for in his closing remarks Hall allows that excluders may be found not only among adjectives, but also among 'nouns and other parts of speech.'[45] The questions we have to ask of 'exists' therefore are:

- Is it ambiguous?
- Not merely *can* it be defined negatively, but *must* it be so defined?

If 'exists' is to be an excluder, the answer has to be 'yes,' not merely to one of these questions, but to both. If we allow that 'exists' is ambiguous, then the question of its being an excluder will turn on whether '*b* exists' *must* be understood simply in terms of what b is precluded from being, i.e., in terms of what b is not. No matter how different the context, '*b* exists' could *only* be understood negatively, e.g., as '*b* is not-fictional,' '*b* is not-dead,' '*b* is not-illusory,' '*b* is not-mythical,' or '*b* is not-nonexistent.'

The simplest case to consider is the last. We might envisage a seer predicting that in two years a son would be born to parents c and d, and that he would be called 'Socrates.' When the prediction was fulfilled, we might imagine the seer announcing triumphantly 'At last Socrates exists, just as I said he would.' If 'exists' were an excluder, then the *only* way of understanding the seer would be as excluding

---

45. Ibid., 7, where he notes: 'Examples would be *choice, intuition, luck.*'

some property from Socrates; and in this case the property excluded would be that of nonexistence. As said by the seer, therefore, 'At last Socrates exists' could only mean 'At last Socrates is not-nonexistent.' If he really were to mean that, we should be entitled to ask him just when Socrates could ever have been said to be nonexistent, i.e., never to have existed. In fact, before Socrates existed he could not even have been referred to, and hence at that time nothing at all could have been attributed to him, not even the Cambridge property of being nonexistent. Thus, it would be impossible for 'At last Socrates exists' to mean 'At last Socrates is no longer nonexistent.' Consequently, 'exists' could not be an excluder, for there was no property for it to exclude.

Still, in other contexts 'Socrates exists' might be proposed as meaning 'Socrates is not-dead' or 'Socrates is not fictional,' and 'exists' as excluding from Socrates the properties of being dead and being fictional respectively. The first case can scarcely be evidence for 'exists' being an excluder, for 'is dead' is itself to be understood as 'is no longer alive.' If it were evidence for anything, it would be for 'exists' as a synonym for 'is alive,' except that 'The Euston Arch no longer exists' could hardly be understood as 'The Euston Arch is no longer alive.'

As for 'Socrates is not fictional' ('Socrates is not a fictional character' would be better), it could support the claim that 'exists' is an excluder only if Socrates really could have been a fictional character. That, however, could have occurred only if a fictional character could be the same person as a real-life one, something which I have argued elsewhere is impossible, even though it is entirely possible that a real-life character should *satisfy the description* of a fictional one.[46] Precisely the same point can be made about any attempt to depict 'exists' as excluding 'is mythical.' Since Socrates never *could* have been either a fictional or mythical character, there is nothing for 'exists' to exclude. That is not to claim that it is wrong to say 'Socrates is not fictional' or 'Socrates is not mythical,' but only that it is misleading to construe those propositions as 'Socrates is not-fictional' and 'Socrates is not-mythical' rather than as 'Not (Socrates is fictional)'

---

46. B. Miller, 'Could any Fictional Character Ever Be Actual?' *Southern Journal of Philosophy* 23 (1985): 325–35.

and 'Not (Socrates is mythical).' From all this it is clear enough that the answer to whether 'exists' must be defined negatively is that it need *not* be. For that reason 'exists' cannot be an excluder.

Either a Predicate Variable or a Disjunction of Predicates? Here we are offered two ways of construing 'exists.' According to one suggestion, it is to be construed as a predicate variable, in which case '*b* exists' would be rendered as '*b* has some property or other' or '($\exists P$)(P is had by b),' where 'P' is a predicate variable. According to the other suggestion, 'exists' would be construed as a disjunction of predicates, in which case '*b* exists' might be rendered as '*b* is F or G or H,' where 'F', 'G', and 'H' are first-level predicates. On either suggestion the result would be to disqualify existence from being an irreducible property of b. In the first case, although b might be allowed to have the properties referred to by whatever predicates may be substituted for 'P', it would have no irreducibly existential predicate. Similarly in the second case: although b might have one of the properties F, G, and H, it would have no property of existence.

Now, if the first suggestion were correct, 'Socrates does not exist' could be rendered as 'Socrates has no properties.' Likewise, if the second suggestion were correct, 'Socrates does not exist' could be rendered as 'Socrates has neither F, nor G, nor H,' i.e., 'Socrates has no properties.' In either case, therefore, 'Socrates does not exist' is to be understood either as 'Socrates has no properties' or as 'There are no properties which Socrates has.'[47] If these propositions are to be interchangeable with 'Socrates does not exist,' however, the former and the latter must mutually entail each other. But do they? According to the view under consideration, 'Socrates does not exist' does indeed entail 'There are no properties which Socrates has.' Unfortunately, however, there is no converse entailment, for 'There are no properties which Socrates has' entails *more than* 'Socrates does not exist.' The reason is that a proposition like 'There are no properties which Socrates has' is precisely what would be meant by calling Socrates a bare particular. Consequently, what is entailed by 'There

---

47. It might be objected that, since Socrates' nonexistence explains its lack of properties, it cannot be analyzed in terms of that lack. That has force, however, only if 'Socrates does not exist' is taken as a tensed proposition rather than as a tenseless one (as it often is).

are no properties which Socrates has' is not a simple proposition but the disjunction '*Either* (Socrates does not exist) *or* (Socrates does exist, but as a bare particular).' This point is a purely logical one, and holds quite independently of how improbable bare particulars might be. However, since the required mutual entailment fails, 'Socrates exists' can be rendered neither by 'Socrates has some property or other' nor by 'Socrates is either *F* or *G* or *H*.'

III. 'Exists' Is Predicable of Individuals

C. J. F. Williams once asked to be shown examples 'usable outside of philosophy' of 'exists' being predicated of individuals.[48] One might have thought that 'Socrates no longer exists,' 'Socrates might not have existed,' 'Joseph is not and Simeon is not,' and 'Before Abraham was, I am' filled the bill to perfection. Not so. These he disqualified not because they had no use outside of philosophy but because of his conviction that they simply could not be employing 'exists' as a first-level predicate. Almost the entire chapter has therefore been devoted to assessing and finally rejecting all such reasons, which might be classified as follows:

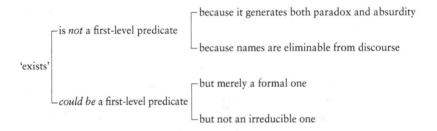

The first, and dominant, objections were those based on the putative paradox and absurdity generated by singular negative existential propositions. As we saw, they fed on two assumptions. The

---

48. C. J. F. Williams, *What Is Existence?*, 79.

first was that it is not enough for proper names to have a reference, they must have a bearer as well. The second was that to admit existence as a real property would be to admit that nonexistence, too, was a real property. Both assumptions proved to be untenable.

The second kind of objection attempted to show, after the manner of Russell and Quine, that proper names were eliminable from our discourse. As a consequence, 'exists' would have been deprived of any term to which it could be attached to form a singular proposition, thereby making a first-level use of 'exists' utterly redundant. In the event, this argument was no more successful than the argument from paradox and absurdity. Nor, indeed, was it possible to argue against a first-level use on the ground that first-level predicates are necessarily equivocal with respect to second-level ones. That ground was undermined by the counter-example of 'disappears.'

Given that a first-level use of 'exists' could not be denied, the next best thing for critics was to limit the damage from that admission by attempting to sanitize it in various ways. One was to argue that, although there was admittedly such a predicate, it was merely a formal one; and what could be more innocuous than a formal predicate? An alternative was to allow that, even if not a formal predicate, it was still quite innocuous since it was reducible to other predicates about which there was none of the controversy that surrounded 'exists.' These attempts at sanitizing or neutering the first-level use of 'exists' were unsuccessful. In fact they were quite unnecessary, for the dreaded paradox and absurdity had proved to be illusory, and attempts to eliminate proper names were notably unsuccessful.

Having begun this chapter by offering propositions purporting to be examples of 'exists' or 'is' as predicates of individuals, I conclude that they cannot be argued away but are precisely what they purport to be. The supposedly dire consequences of accepting them at face value have proved to be entirely fanciful, and their suggested reparsings have been not only counter-intuitive but unnecessary as well.

One might therefore think that there was no longer any reason to deny that 'exists' was in fact predicable of concrete individuals. There are, however, two quite powerful incentives to do just that. One is the seemingly obvious point that existence could be a real property of an individual only if there were some individual for it to be a property of, i.e., only if an individual had some actuality in its own right, quite independently of its property of existence. Less crucial, but not to be taken lightly, is the contention that existence could be a real property only if it 'added' something to individuals—which it clearly does not. I address both difficulties in chapter 4. Prior to that, however, I shall need to explain something of the metaphysics underpinning that rebuttal, as well as to show that existence is a real property, not merely a Cambridge one.

Appendix to Chapter Two

Zalta and Parsons on Distinguishing 'Exists' from 'Is'

Chapter 2 distinguished sharply between the uses of 'exists' as a first-level predicate and as a second-level predicate. In regard to the first-level use, it drew no distinction between 'exists' and an existential use of 'is.' Precisely such a distinction, however, has been introduced in the work of Terence Parsons[1] and Edward N. Zalta[2] who draw to some extent on the work of Meinong, and whose aim has been to provide a logic—an intensional logic—which will explain the apparent failure of one or other principles of non-intensional logic in certain contexts. Expressed otherwise, their goal has been to 'explain how common sense non-existence claims of natural language mean what they seem to mean and have the truth-values, logical form, and entailments that they seem to have.'[3]

---

1. T. Parsons, *Nonexistent Objects* (New Haven: Yale University Press, 1980). Parsons was influenced not only by Meinong but by the seminal work of Richard Routley (now, Sylvan) in his unpublished but widely read 'Exploring Meinong's Jungle.'

2. E. Zalta, *Intentional Logic and the Metaphysics of Intentionality* (Cambridge: MIT Press, 1988).

3. Ibid., 103.

Whereas I have been concerned solely with 'exists' (or 'is') in relation to *concrete* individuals, Parsons and Zalta have been concerned also with its possible relation to numbers, universal properties, propositions, and such intensional entities as Pegasus, Sherlock Holmes, unicorns, round squares, and golden mountains. Although such entities are of considerable interest in their own right, my only point in examining them here is to determine whether they add anything to what we already know about the first-level use of 'exists,' i.e., as predicable of concrete individuals.

The system advocated by Parsons has three basic features:

- *The distinction between nuclear and extra-nuclear predicates and likewise between their corresponding properties.* As examples of nuclear predicates we are offered 'is blue,' 'is tall,' 'kicked Socrates,' 'was kicked by Socrates,' 'kicked something,' 'is golden,' 'is a mountain.' Examples of extra-nuclear predicates include 'exists,' 'is mythical,' 'is fictional,' 'is possible,' 'is impossible,' 'is thought about by Meinong,' 'is worshipped by someone,' 'is complete.' As critics have noted, the distinction is far from transparent.
- *The correlation between non-empty sets of nuclear properties and genuine objects.* Objects are correlated with (but not identified with) sets of nuclear properties—existent objects with complete sets, and nonexistent objects with incomplete sets. A set is complete if, for any nuclear property, an object has that property or its negation. Otherwise, a set is incomplete. Critics consider this distinction, too, to be less than obvious. Moreover, the stipulation that no two objects have exactly the same nuclear properties might suggest that Parsons adheres to the suspect Identity of Indiscernibles.
- *The distinction between objects that 'are' and objects that 'exist.'* The predicate 'exists' is said to be applicable to 'all the ordinary [concrete] objects that we normally take to exist.'[4] Parsons, however, also recognizes objects that would not normally be regarded as concrete, namely, golden mountains, winged horses, round squares, Pegasus, and Sherlock Holmes. These objects are said

---

4. Parsons, *Nonexistent Objects*, 11.

not to exist but merely *to be*. Thus, of objects like tables we can say both 'Tables exist' and 'There exist tables.' Of other objects we can say merely that there are such things, e.g., 'There are unicorns.' Such objects are said to be *nonexistent*. In virtue of the distinction between *existing* and merely *being* it is then possible to say without any kind of contradiction, or even paradox, 'There are unicorns, but they do not exist.' This makes perfectly good sense because, as Parsons uses the terms 'is' and 'exist,' what exists does not exhaust what there is.[5]

Obviously, this is directly at odds with the Frege-Russell-Quine view of existence, according to which what exists is precisely what there is. Less obviously, perhaps, and despite its distinction between what exists and what there is, the theory of Parsons sits uneasily with the two-sense theory of 'exists' as well, for the latter theory presupposes an absolute distinction between individuals and properties, a distinction which is blurred by Parsons. Even if we allow that his *existing* objects are not mere bundles or sets of properties, it is not obvious how the same can be said of his nonexistent objects. He needs therefore to tell us in what sense the golden mountain is anything more than a set of properties, namely, of being golden, of being a mountain, and of being existent. If it is nothing more than such a set, it is no more concrete than are properties; and these he has classed as abstract. Contrary to his declared aim, therefore, his theory would seem not to be one about concrete objects after all. But if it is not about concrete objects, 'is existent' cannot be a first-level predicate—unlike 'is golden' and 'is a mountain.' But, then, what becomes of the claim that existence and being existent are two kinds of being? They can hardly be two kinds of being if the former is a first-level property while the latter is merely a second-level one.

Zalta, comparing his own theory with that of Parsons, draws attention to its 'explanatory elegance' in replying to Russell's three objections against Meinong.[6] Whereas each reply by Parsons to those objections employs a different strategy, Zalta employs precisely the same two hypotheses in each of his replies:

---

5. Ibid., 5.
6. Zalta, *Intentional Logic*, 134.

- That 'is' can also be read as 'encodes.'
- That descriptions of the form 'The $G_1, \ldots, G_n$,' when said in a Meinongian way, have readings in which they denote A-objects that encode the properties $G_1, \ldots, G_n$.

The notions of A-objects (abstract objects) and of encoding are central to his theory, and need now to be explained.

One of the problems with intentional objects is that they themselves do not seem to have the properties that they represent—the object which represents blue is not itself blue. Although this was a point to which Brentano adverted in the last century, its history extends as far as the Middle Ages and beyond to Aristotle. The medievals resolved their difficulty by suggesting that the identical form may have two modes of existence, physical and intentional. For example, the identical form or forms had materially (physically) by Bucephalus would be had immaterially (intentionally) by the person perceiving him. All the forms (substantial and accidental alike) existing physically in Bucephalus would exist intentionally in whoever perceived him.

To deal with the same problem, Zalta distinguishes not between physical and intentional *existence* but between physical and intentional *objects*. Physical objects are said to be concrete and to *exemplify* various properties. Intentional objects, on the contrary, are abstract, a term which Zalta seems to regard as synonymous with 'non-spatiotemporal.' These A-objects, as he calls them, fail to exemplify those properties at all but do, however, *encode* them. As he notes, the distinction between exemplifying and encoding properties is due to Ernst Mally. Abstract objects have content not by exemplifying properties but only by encoding them. Abstract objects that encode properties serve two purposes:

- They serve as intentional objects of states directed towards non-existents.
- They also serve to characterize and reify the content of mental representations.[7]

Zalta's reasoning for A-objects would seem to be:

---

7. Ibid., 5.

- There must be some way or other in which the golden mountain *has* the properties of being golden and being a mountain.
- But, in the case of the golden mountain, 'having those properties' cannot be understood as 'exemplifying those properties.'
- Therefore, there must be some way of having properties which neither is nor entails exemplifying them.
- Call this other way 'encoding.' And call the object which encodes properties an *abstract* one. Let concrete objects be said to *exist,* and abstract objects be said not to exist but merely to *be.*

Although it is clear what encoding is meant to achieve, it is not quite so clear what it actually is—no more clear, it would seem, than the medieval notion of intentional existence, nor any more clear than the nuclear/extra-nuclear distinction drawn by Parsons.

Why draw the 'exists'/'is' distinction? Because it seems intuitively clear that 'Pegasus,' 'Zeus,' and 'Hamlet' are names of nonexistent, mythical, and fictional creatures. After all, 'the logic of natural language seems to presuppose that it makes sense to refer to and talk about these creatures.'[8] Indeed, if 'Quine were right when he says that "Hamlet doesn't exist" means "~$(\exists x)(x = h)$", then "Hamlet" would fail to denote,' and that would make quite mysterious the natural inference from 'John's paper is about Hamlet' to 'John's paper is about something.'[9] Consequently, there would seem to be a case for not dismissing Pegasus and others as complete nonentities, but for admitting that they do have some kind of entity. One might even be tempted to say that they exist, except that this could be taken to imply that they were no less real than Aristotle, Plato, and Julius Caesar, which few would be prepared to accept.

To do justice to the foregoing considerations, therefore, we are urged to allow that Pegasus and Zeus truly *are* (or have being), but not to go so far as to accept that they *exist* (or have existence). For Zalta, 'is' or 'being' is represented by '$\exists$' and is called 'logical or metaphysical existence,' while existing is called 'physical existence' and 'exists' is represented by 'E!' It is with the aid of this distinction between existing and being that Zalta develops an intensional logic

---

8. Ibid., 103.
9. Ibid., 104.

which handles intentional objects with a facility not to be found in non-intensional logics.

The relative positions of Parsons and Zalta on 'exists' and 'is' can be summarized as follows:

1. *Parsons:* Distinguishes 'exists' from 'is,' existence from being. Both 'exists' and 'is' are first-level predicates, since each is said of concrete objects, the former of complete objects and the latter of incomplete. Indeed, Parsons explicitly denies that 'is' should be rendered as '∃.'[10]

2. *Zalta:* Likewise distinguishes 'exists' from 'is,' existence from being. 'Exists' ('E!') is a first-level predicate. However, 'is' is predicated of abstract entities and, contrary to Parsons, is represented by '∃,' which would indicate that it is a second-level predicate.

It is no part of this book to discuss the relative merits of Frege-Russell logic (perhaps augmented by suggestions from the likes of Howell[11] and van Inwagen[12]) vs. intensional logics, nor the merits of the intensional proposals of Parsons vs. those of Zalta. It was of some interest, however, to discover whether the new use proposed for 'is' impacts at all on what we know of the first-level use of 'exists.' It appears not, for that use of 'exists' is as predicable of concrete individuals (complete entities). In Zalta's use of 'is,' however, it is predicable not of concrete entities but of abstract ones. According to Parsons, it is predicable not of complete entities but only of incomplete ones. Moreover, it must be said that these incomplete entities appear to be no more concrete than are properties.

It emerges, then, that neither Zalta's use of 'is' nor that of Parsons adds anything to what has been said in chapter 2 about 'exists' as predicable of concrete individuals. That, of course, is not to take anything away from their noteworthy contribution to intensional logic.

---

10. Ibid., 6.

11. R. Howell, 'Fictional Objects: How They Are and How They Aren't,' *Poetics* 8 (1979): 129–77.

12. P. van Inwagen, 'Creatures of Fiction,' *American Philosophical Quarterly* 14 (1977): 299–308.

three

Existence—A Real Property, but of What Kind?

Since 'exists' is predicable of individuals, it follows that existence is a property of individuals. I say that because I take properties to be whatever is attributed to something by a predicate. The question to be answered therefore is whether existence is a real or a Cambridge property. To accept it as real would be to provoke the apparently compelling objection from Hume and Kant mentioned at the end of the last chapter and quoted in chapter 1, namely, that existence should presumably make some 'addition' to individuals—which it manifestly does not. To come to grips with that objection, we'll need first to know what kind of entity Socrates' existence is—a property or a property instance. The answer will determine the kind of relation that Socrates bears to his existence, which is central to the next chapter. And, once that relation is known, it will become clear how his instance of existence can be attributed to him without, indeed, adding anything to him.

However, I run ahead of myself, for the goals of the present chapter are limited first to determining whether Socrates' existence is a real property or merely a Cambridge one, and then to considering whether his existence is a property or a property instance. As a prelude to addressing that question, I should set out the rationale for the metaphysics employed in answering it. Hence the following sections in the chapter:

- Whether Socrates' existence is a real property.
- The metaphysical underpinning to be employed.
- Socrates' existence is a property instance.

I. Existence a Real Property

From the preceding chapter it might be recalled that Williams would have had no objection to existence being merely a Cambridge property. What so disquieted him was the suggestion of its being a real one, for that was thought to conjure up such visions as sheep farmers 'searching for the stigmata of existence,' and horticulturalists being obliged 'to examine several specimens of blue buttercup before concluding that there were none.'

As we saw, the alleged absurdity stemmed from the misguided assumption that existence could not be a real property unless nonexistence too were real. It was misguided because it was a non sequitur to argue from existence being a real property to the conclusion that *non*existence likewise should be a real property. That sufficed to dispose of the dreaded absurdity, and thus to remove one of the prime arguments against existence being a real property. Still, that was not yet enough, since it merely countered considerations *against* existence being a real property without, however, offering any argument *for* its being a real property. I therefore suggest the following argument:

- Properties of individuals are either accidental or essential.
- If accidental, they are either real or Cambridge.
- If Cambridge, they are merely relational, either overtly or covertly.
- But the referent of 'exists' in 'Nelson Mandela exists' (namely, his existence) is an accidental property of an individual, though *not* a relational one.
- Therefore, it is not a Cambridge property.
- But if it is an accidental property yet not a Cambridge one, it is real.

- Therefore, Nelson Mandela's existence is a real property of him and, in general, any concrete individual's existence is a real property of it.[1]

In regard to the first premiss, it should be noted that typical Cambridge properties are the referents of relational predicates one place of which has been filled by a singular term. Examples are 'is taller than Bill,' 'is observed by Maria,' 'is heard by Judith.' It might be objected, however, that not all Cambridge properties are the referents of relational (multi-place) predicates, for being famous, being sought after, and being hated are Cambridge properties despite being referents of ostensibly one-place predicates, namely, 'is famous,' 'is sought after,' and 'is hated.'

Being famous, however, is the property of being highly esteemed by innumerable people, and hence is in fact a covert relation between the object of esteem and those who esteem it. Moreover, although esteeming Socrates is a real property, *being* esteemed is merely a Cambridge one, for a person may be esteemed even if completely oblivious of the fact. Similarly with the properties of being loved, hated, understood, sought after, and so on. All of them are not only relational but also Cambridge properties of the objects of those attitudes.

Doubtless, this might be challenged on the grounds that the *effects* of being loved, hated, understood, and sought after are sometimes disturbingly real. Quite so: those effects are undoubtedly real. They are not, however, effects of the properties just mentioned, none of which need produce any effect at all. One can be loved, hated, understood, and sought after without having the faintest idea of being the object of these attitudes, and hence can be quite unaffected by them. Whatever effects may ensue come not from being loved,

---

1. Since it is commonly thought that existence could be a real predicate only if it added something to an individual, it is noteworthy that this argument makes no appeal to any such premiss. In fact, it is false, as I argue in chapter 4, section IV.

hated, understood, and sought after, but from the quite different properties of *knowing* that one is loved, *knowing* that one is hated, *knowing* that one is understood, and *knowing* that one is sought after. It is these properties that are real, not those of being loved, hated, understood, and sought after: the latter are purely Cambridge and, in the absence of such knowledge, are not even coincident with any effects, let alone their cause.

In regard to the fourth premiss I should note that, in speaking of Nelson Mandela's existence, I am speaking of contingent existence, and my point is that it is not to be construed in terms of a relation to other contingent beings.[2] I merely observe, therefore, that the universe as a whole can be said to exist, despite its having no relation whatever to any other spatiotemporal entities. If it be objected that the universe as a whole might be related in some non-causal way to other universes, the reply is that even the totality of all universes (should there be more than one) can equally be said to exist. And, ex hypothesi, *that* totality would not be related to any other spatiotemporal entity whether causally or non-causally. Consequently, existence is not a relational property.

There is, however, a possible objection to this conclusion. Peter Forrest has pointed out that, even if existence is not a relation between *co*-existing entities, someone might suggest that it is a relation between *successively* existing entities, namely, between successive time-slices. On this view, it would be merely a *façon de parler* to speak of entities as existing for five minutes or five centuries. More accurately, they should be said to exist at every moment within five minutes or five centuries as the case may be. Since there are no moments except in relation to other moments, there could be no existence except in relation to prior and/or succeeding moments of existence. On this reasoning, therefore, existence would be an essentially relational property, and thus a merely Cambridge property.

Not so; for it could also be argued by parity of reasoning that even a property like blue could be analyzed in terms of relations, al-

---

2. This leaves open the question of whether his existence may or may not be dependent on a creator, since I take it that a creator would not be a contingent being, but a necessary one.

beit spatial ones. Thus, one might argue that a surface is blue only if every point in a given area of it is blue. Of course, there is no such thing as a point except in relation to other points. Hence, there could be no property of being blue except in relation to prior and/or posterior points of blue. Being blue should therefore be analyzable in terms of the relations of (spatial) priority and posteriority. But this argument is surely unsound, since being blue is precisely the kind of property that cannot be analyzed in such terms. The argument for existence being analyzable in terms of (temporal) priority and posteriority is therefore no less unsound: it provides no reason to deny that existence is a real entity. But just what kind of entity would it be, a property or a property instance?

II. Metaphysical Underpinnings

Before responding to the foreshadowed questions, I should explain that this book might well qualify as an essay in what Strawson called 'descriptive metaphysics,' namely, an attempt to describe something of the actual categorial structure of the world.[3] It thus differs from the so-called 'revisionary metaphysics' which, in Strawson's view, is concerned to offer a better structure. Presumably, an example of a better structure would be one that embraced one or all such entities as Propositions, possible worlds, and haecceities. Although I certainly hold no brief for entities of that kind, I should stress that in this book I need not argue against them, since they do not clash with the various metaphysical positions upon which I shall be relying.

In seeking to describe something of the actual categorial structure of the world, I shall be following Frege in maintaining the priority of linguistic categories over ontological ones. This is simply the claim that the categories of the things we talk about are to be determined by the linguistic categories of the language we employ to speak

---

3. It was in the Preface to his *Individuals* (London: Methuen, 1959) that Strawson drew this by now familiar distinction. 'Descriptive metaphysics' is an unfortunate term, however, for it suggests a metaphysics that makes no intellectual demands on its practitioners, a suggestion that could not be further from the truth.

about them. In other words, the way in which the world is sliced up mirrors the way in which our language is sliced up by logical analysis. Linguistic categories, of course, are not to be confused with grammatical ones. Rather, they are those revealed by the logical analysis of language into, for example, proper names, first-level predicates, second-level predicates, functional expressions, and so on. The corresponding ontological categories are those of object, first-level property, second-level property, and function, respectively.

Thus, an entity is an object (whether concrete or abstract) precisely because it can be referred to by an expression that functions as a proper name: Socrates qualifies as an object because he can be referred to by a name, not vice versa. Likewise, it is because predicates are attachable to proper names that an object can be said to possess (first-level) properties: being wise is a property because it is what the predicate in such propositions as 'Socrates is wise' stands for. Hence, on the Fregean view, the ontological category of 'object' reflects the linguistic category of 'proper name' rather than vice versa. Similarly, the ontological category of 'first-level property' reflects the linguistic category of 'first-level predicate': it is the latter that determines what entities are first-level properties. This is far from being a form of idealism, however, for it is not saying that external reality (objects, properties, and the like) is *constituted* by language. It is saying, rather, that those entities are *apprehended* via (the logical analysis of) language.

Unsurprisingly, there may be some initial resistance to this view and a preference for its converse, namely, the view that linguistic categories reflect ontological ones—that the linguistic expressions in 'Socrates is wise' are to be assigned their roles in accordance with the ontological categories exemplified in a wise Socrates. On that view, 'Socrates' would be a proper name because it stands for an object, and 'is wise' would be a predicate because it stands for a property.

To test that view, let us suppose it to be correct. To do so would be to suppose that someone could be quite clear about the ontological categories exemplified by a wise Socrates (namely, object and property), but quite at a loss to know which of them 'Socrates' would stand for and which 'is wise' would stand for. To say that someone was at a loss to know what each of 'Socrates' and 'is wise' would stand for, however, would be to say that one was helpless to say how those expressions functioned in the language, helpless in seeking to assign their linguistic roles. But for a person ignorant of such basic linguistic functions, it would be impossible to say which was which among the ontological categories exemplified by a wise Socrates. Since that flies completely in the face of our initial supposition, however, it is a supposition that must be abandoned.

The upshot is that the logical category to which an expression belongs must be determined not by the ontological category of what the expression stands for, but by the way in which it is employed in the language.[4] It is for this reason that I atttach such metaphysical significance to the logical structure of language. Only by determining the logical status of an expression is it then possible to determine the correlative ontological category of what the expression stands for. As Dummett has remarked, 'language may be a distorting mirror, but it is the only mirror we have.'[5]

That 'linguistic mirror' will be crucial in the following section where the task will be to determine whether Socrates' existence is a universal property or a property instance—a complete entity or an incomplete one.[6] The answer will turn first on Frege's view that predicates are incomplete *expressions* and, second, on his view that their referents are, correspondingly, incomplete *entities*. More particularly, if we want to know about the incompleteness of what he called concepts (properties), it is incumbent upon us to examine the incompleteness of the expressions that refer to them, namely, predicates. I shall therefore be concerned with the incompleteness of predicates, from which it will be a simple step to conclude to the correlative incompleteness of properties, and hence to the recognition of property *instances*. That is the nub of the argument for acknowledging the ontological status of property instances.

---

4. Cf. M. Dummett, *Frege, Philosophy of Language,* 2nd ed. (London: Duckworth, 1981), 35–38.

5. M. Dummett, *Origins of Analytical Philosophy* (Cambridge: Harvard University Press, 1993), 6. This would be contested by Peacock and Evans in their support for the priority of thought over language as the ultimate 'mirror.'

6. Cf. M. Dummett, *Frege, Philosophy of Language,* 170–79, 471–74.

III. Socrates' Existence Is a Property Instance

The notion of property instances is not new in the history of philosophy. Indeed, Aristotelian scholars have debated whether such entities are any part of Aristotle's ontology. Many think they are, but many others think not. Even the latter, however, have no difficulty in understanding the notion of these entities whose existence they deny, and which have sometimes been called individualized forms. To introduce them, I begin by contrasting them with tropes, a rather more contemporary kind of entity which few profess to find unintelligible, not even the many who cannot accept them. Keith Campbell describes them as follows:

> Consider . . . the instance of a property (as we might call it) in some concrete particular, say a particular shape that this very lollipop has, or the specific colour that is present here, in this place at this time. Or the specimen of flavour which it has. This case of shape, this specimen of colour, this instance of flavour can and should be taken as beings *in their own right*. They are indeed the elements of being.
>
> They are particulars; that is, they exist at one definite place in space at any one time. They are not multiple like universals. They are not fully present in indefinitely many locations, but precisely one. The (instance of) colour in one lollipop is a different item from the (instance of) colour in a second lollipop, even if the lollipops are just the same shade of red. And this numerical difference is the characteristic mark of a particular. These particulars are clearly not ordinary things like shoes and ships.[7] [They are called 'tropes.']

7. K. Campbell, *Metaphysics: An Introduction* (Encino: Dickinson, 1976), 212. Emphasis mine. Trope theory has been proposed by G. F. Stout, *Studies in Philosophy and Psychology* (London: Macmillan, 1930); D. C. Williams, 'On the Elements of Being I & II,' *Review of Metaphysics* 7 (1943–44): 1–18 and 171–92; K. Campbell, 'The Metaphysics of Abstract Individuals,' *Midwest Studies in Philosophy* 6 (1981), 477–88, and *Abstract Particulars* (Oxford: Blackwell, 1990); J. Bacon, *Universals and Property Instances: The Alphabet of Being* (Oxford: Blackwell, 1995).

Clearly, the notion of a trope rather turns on its head the Platonic view according to which properties like Socrates' wisdom have to be understood in terms of an abstract universal entity, Wisdom, which is exemplified in Socrates. In trope theory, however, there is in Socrates a *particular* entity which is this instance of wisdom (a trope), and is quite distinct from the wisdom trope had by Aristotle. Moreover, the 'universal' Wisdom would be the set of all the wisdom tropes, and hence ontologically posterior to them. D. C. Williams called tropes 'the primary constituents of this or any possible world, the alphabet of being.'[8] In the absence of any wisdom tropes there would be no universal Wisdom.

The individualized forms that some ascribe to Aristotle[9] are like tropes to a limited extent, for they too could be described as 'this shape, this specimen of colour, this instance of flavour,' as is evident in Elizabeth Anscombe's interpretation of Aristotle:

> [An] example which he gives of what is found in a subject, but not predicated of it, is 'the white'. That is to say, he regards e.g. *the white of this paper* as a particular, just as it is natural to regard *the surface of this paper* as a particular. This is not his

---

8. D. C. Williams, 'On the Elements of Being I & II,' 7.

9. Those ascribing this view to Aristotle include J. L. Ackrill, *Aristotle's Categories and De Interpretatione* (Oxford: Oxford University Press, 1974), 74; R. E. Allen, 'Individual Properties in Aristotle's Categories,' *Phronesis* 14 (1969): 31–39; G. E. M. Anscombe, *Three Philosophers* (Oxford: Blackwell, 1969), 8–10; H. Granger, 'A Defense of the Traditional Position Concerning Aristotle's Non-substantial Particulars,' *Canadian Journal of Philosophy* 10 (1980): 593–606; M. J. Woods, 'Problems in *Metaphysics Z,*' chapter 13 in J. M. Moravscik, ed., *Aristotle: A Collection of Critical Essays* (New York: Doubleday, 1967), 215–38; R. Albritton, 'Forms of Particular Substances in Aristotle's Metaphysics,' *Journal of Philosophy* 54 (1957): 694–703. Those denying the foregoing view include G. E. L. Owen, 'Inherence,' *Phronesis* 10 (1965): 97–105; M. Frede, *Essays in Ancient Philosophy* (Oxford: Oxford University Press, 1987), chap. 4; M. Loux, *Primary Ousia* (Ithaca: Cornell University Press, 1991). R. Dancy is 'also inclined to adopt Owen's view' in his 'On Some of Aristotle's Thoughts about Substances,' *Philosophical Review* 84 (1975): 354.

In *Three Philosophers* (Oxford: Blackwell, 1969), 79–81, P. T. Geach argues that Aquinas supported the notion of individualized forms.

language; as I remarked, his 'individuals,'—*atoma*—are usually substances and he uses no other word as I am using 'particular'. But in one place at least (*Categories* 1b 6–8) his language implies that there are *atoma,* other than substances, which are not *predicable of* anything. If so, it seems legitimate to apply the word 'particular' so as to cover both individual substances and these other entities which are found in them.[10]

This passage illustrates not only the similarity between individualized forms and tropes but also the quite radical difference between them. Tropes, as Campbell reminds us, should be taken as 'beings in their own right,' and for that reason might presumably be regarded as 'little substances.' Individualized forms are most certainly not beings in their own right, not little substances at all. While the white of this paper and the surface of this paper are genuine particulars, they are also quite inseparable from the individuals (primary substances) to which they belong and in which, according to some, Aristotle says they inhere.

Trope theory differs from this interpretation of Aristotle in yet another way, for the former depicts tropes as logically prior to universals, no matter whether the latter are thought to exist *extra rem* as in Plato or *in re* as in Aristotle. The individualized forms sometimes ascribed to Aristotle, however, do not purport to be logically prior to universals, either *in re* or *extra rem*. They are, in fact, quite compatible with either kind of universal, and compatible too with universals not being entities of any kind but merely notions.

The entities which I have introduced as individualized forms are what I shall henceforth call 'property instances.' More needs to be said about them, however, to sharpen their distinction from substances or even the 'little substances' of trope theory. How are they to be understood if they are as distinct from each other as are tropes, but yet not so distinct as to be entities in their own right, as tropes are said to be? The brief answer, upon which I shall elaborate shortly, turns on the Fregean distinction between complete entities and incomplete entities. Both individuals (primary substances) and tropes are complete entities—entities in their own right. Property instances,

---

10. G. E. M. Anscombe and P. T. Geach, *Three Philosophers,* 9. Emphasis in the original.

however, have not the slightest claim to being complete entities, which is of course far from saying that they are not entities in any sense at all. They are entities, indeed, but only incomplete ones; they are entities not in their own right, but only to the extent that they are completed by complete entities. As noted earlier, it is the *entire* being of an incomplete entity like a property 'to be *of* an object, [and] of a relation to be *between* two objects.'[11]

Argument for Property Instances

I hold no brief for trope theory, and have in fact argued that it has the unfortunate consequence of allowing individuals—which ex hypothesi are not instantiable in other individuals—to be instantiable in them after all.[12] Still, there is something appealing in Campbell's claim that there are 'this case of shape, this specimen of odour, this instance of flavour' though, I hasten to add, nothing at all appealing about his further claim that they are beings in their own right. There is something appealing, too, in Aristotle's speaking of the white of this paper as a particular. Still, whatever their initial appeal, these examples are far from constituting any sort of ostensive argument for property instances. However, I do have a *non*-ostensive argument that may be set out as follows.

3.1   First-level properties are the ontological correlates of first-level predicates.

3.2   But, first-level predicates are incomplete *expressions*— expressions that cannot be isolated from the propositions in which they occur.

3.3   Therefore, first-level properties are incomplete *entities*— entities that cannot be isolated from the individuals to which they belong

3.4   But to say that an entity cannot be isolated from the individual to which it belongs is to say that it is a property instance.

---

11. M. Dummett, *Frege, Philosophy of Language*, 176. For more on this topic, see 174–79, 257–62, and 471–74 of the same work.

12. 'Individuals and Individuality,' *Grazer Philosophische Studien* 37 (1990): 75–91.

Premiss (3.1) is simply part of what I have been explaining in the previous section.

In support of premiss (3.2): On a Fregean view, the relation between name and predicate in an atomic proposition is one of complete expression to incomplete expression. The notion of incompleteness or unsaturatedness is, however, a difficult one, so much so that Frege himself confessed to being unable to define it, and concluded that he must confine himself 'to hinting at what I have in mind by means of a metaphorical expression; and here I rely on my reader's agreeing to meet me half way.'[13] In regard to the incompleteness of predicates, however, Geach has gone well beyond merely 'hinting' at how it is to be understood, as will now be evident.

I begin by noting that a predicate is an incomplete expression not simply in virtue of its being part of a proposition, for otherwise every logical part of every proposition would be an incomplete expression in the Fregean sense. Clearly, that is not the case; for a proposition itself may be part of a complex proposition, and a name may also be part of a proposition, though neither propositions nor names are incomplete expressions. What, then, does it mean to say that a predicate is incomplete? As Geach has long argued, it means that a predicate is an unquotable, an undetachable expression: although readily *discernible* in propositions, it is nevertheless *not detachable* from them. Such is the incompleteness of a predicate that it cannot even be written down except in writing down the proposition in which it occurs.

Geach insists that, to recognize a predicate that is common to two propositions, it is not enough to recognize merely the *words* they have in common. Rather, one has also to recognize the *pattern* they have in common. The inadequacy of recognizing mere expressions and the correlative need to recognize a pattern is illustrated in his Polish example 'Maria zabiła Jana' ('Mary kills John'), in which the predication is not effected by the bare word 'zabił.' Rather, it is ef-

---

13. G. Frege, 'What Is a Function,' in P. T. Geach and M. Black, *Philosophical Writings of Gottlob Frege* (Oxford: Blackwell, 1960), 115. In 'Concept and Object' (55) he makes the same point: '"Complete" and "unsaturated" are of course only figures of speech; but all that I wish or am able to do here is to give hints.'

fected by the functional expression 'ξ zabił(a) ζ which, as he notes, is shorthand for the following:

> The name ξ in the nominative case, and the name ζ in the accusative case, are combined with a token word 'zabił,' inflected to agree in gender with the name ξ[14]

Perhaps more perspicuous than even Geach's own example is one showing that predicates need not be constituted by words at all, but by nothing more or less than a pattern. For instance, a very limited kind of language might have its names written in lower case, and its predicates indicated by varying the height of one or more letters that compose the names, e.g:

	Possible language	English translation
Name:	'christopher'	'Christopher'
Propositions formed with the name:	'Christopher'	'Christopher is black'
	'cHristopher'	'Christopher is wise'
	'chRisTopher'	'Christopher is angry'

In such cases neither *words* nor inflections are needed even to indicate the presence of a predicate, let alone to constitute one. On the contrary, the predicate would be both indicated and constituted solely by the pattern of letter heights in the inscription of the name.[15] If we think of this example together with the Polish one from Geach, 'surely the temptation vanishes to regard the predicate . . . as a simple sign with its slots for proper names quite external to it.'[16]

---

14. P. T. Geach, 'Names and Identity,' in S. Guttenplan, ed., *Mind and Language* (Oxford: Oxford University Press, 1975), 148.

15. Of course, in order to obtain even a modest range of predicates, the names would need to be reasonably long. Moreover, if Frank Ramsey were right in thinking that names and predicates were interchangeable, then names might be indicated by patterns of letter heights in the inscription of a predicate. The argument in this book, however, is quite neutral as to whether Ramsey is right or wrong, since I assume only that the Fregean analysis is at least one legitimate analysis of atomic propositions.

16. Geach, 'Names and Identity,' 148.

At this point it might be objected that, even if there are some languages in which a predicate cannot be recognized without recognizing a corresponding pattern in a proposition, there are others in which that is patently not the case. Surely the predicate common to 'Socrates is wise' and 'Plato is wise' is nothing but the expression 'is wise.' Surely, there is no need to understand the predicate as conforming to some such instruction as the following:

The name ξ is placed adjacent to, and to the left of, the token phrase 'is wise.'

The answer is that most surely there is indeed such a need. Admittedly, the instruction is both so simple and, to us, so obvious that we may be inclined to discount it as entirely trivial. It may seem that, even without any such instruction, we could perfectly well combine the expressions 'Socrates' and 'is wise' to form the proposition 'Socrates is wise.' That suggestion is of course not totally implausible; for we can readily make sense even of English that has been severely butchered, and we might well understand a foreigner who even reversed the normal word order by uttering 'Is wise Socrates.' However, the intelligibility of butchered English has its limits; and there are many possible patterns that might exceed those limits. A few examples are given below.

A. 'is wise'

's
e
t
a
r
c
o
S'

B.   'is wise'
                                        'Socrates'

C. 'is wise'   'Socrates'

We may be tempted to regard (A), (B), and (C) as 'unnatural' as compared with the 'naturalness' of our present way of writing English. Yet, no one way of writing it is any more natural than the others, as Chinese and Arabic word-orders surely attest. And that should alert us to the fact that, in different circumstances, our present way of writing might have seemed to other people every bit as contrived as (A) seems to us now. Lifelong familiarity with the present pattern exhibited in 'Socrates is wise' should therefore not mislead us into dismissing it as not worth mentioning. Hence, the difference between 'Maria zabiła Jana' and 'Socrates is wise' is not that there is some pattern to the former but none to the latter. Rather, there is a pattern to both: it is simply that it appears to us as more striking in the former but notably less so in the latter. So our earlier conclusion remains intact: predicates cannot be detached from the propositions in which they occur. Although in some languages the *expressions* used in forming predicates can certainly be detached, there are no languages at all in which the *predicates* themselves can be detached or placed within quotation marks.

The predicate in 'Socrates is wise' can be neither 'is wise' nor '___ is wise,' for obviously each of them is what the predicate is not, namely, a quotable expression. On the contrary, the role of 'is wise' is merely to *indicate* or *signal* the presence of a common predicate in 'Socrates is wise' and 'Plato is wise'; the predicate itself, however, is not even a proposition manqué such as 'is wise' might perhaps have been thought to be. It is, as Geach says, simply a feature of, or pattern in, a proposition. Although it is undoubtedly convenient to *represent* it by the expression '___ is wise,' that expression is not a predicate at all but merely an instruction for forming a proposition.

It is now apparent that the union between the logical parts of a proposition is quite unlike that between the parts of a jigsaw puzzle or between a socket and a plug. It is a far more binding union—so binding as to be indissoluble. It is indissoluble precisely because one of the parts (e.g., the predicate in 'Socrates is wise') is not a linguistic entity in its own right but is entirely parasitic upon the proposition in which it occurs, and which truly is a linguistic entity in its own right. It is for just that reason, and in that sense, that the predicate deserves to be called an *incomplete* expression. It is incomplete not in the relatively weak sense in which a wall might be called an incomplete house or a chapter might be called an incomplete story, namely, an isolated fragment of a story. Rather, it is incomplete in the strongest possible sense, namely, that it cannot occur even as an isolated fragment of language. If it does not occur *in* a proposition, it does not occur at all. There is simply no way in which it can be separated from the name that completes it to form the proposition in which it occurs.[17]

I should add that there is nothing unique about predicate incompleteness, for what is true of predicates is equally true of relational and of functional expressions, i.e., of expressions that refer to relations and functions respectively. These, too, are incomplete and are no more quotable or separable from complete expressions than are predicates. About functional expressions, for example, Dummett has noted that 'the only sort of expression by means of which the function can be referred to is a functional expression, an expression, namely, which, being incomplete, *cannot occur on its own, or as a separable part of a sentence.*'[18] He could have said exactly the same of relational expressions.

As mentioned earlier, the discussion of predicate incompleteness was not an end in itself but merely a prerequisite for grasping the incompleteness of first-level *properties.* To recognize the nature of predicate incompleteness is ipso facto to recognize the nature of property incompleteness for, as was argued in regard to premiss (3.1), the latter simply mirrors the former. Since ontological categories should be assigned in accordance with the categories of the logical parts of a proposition, it remains that the logical category to which an expression belongs is determined not by what the expression stands for but, as Dummett has noted, solely by the way in which it is employed in the language.[19] Only by first determining the way in which it is employed in language is it then possible to determine the appropriate ontological category pertaining to what the expression stands for.

---

17. Of course, it is only in atomic propositions that it is completed by a *name.* In propositions like '$(\exists x)(x$ is a man$)$' or '$(\exists x)(x$ is a man $\supset x$ is wise$)$' the completion is performed by the second-level predicates '$(\exists x)(x$ ___$)$' in the former and by '$(\exists x)(x$ ___ $\supset x$ ___$)$' in the latter.

18. M. Dummett, *Frege, Philosophy of Language,* 176. My emphasis.

19. Ibid., 57.

Let us now apply these remarks to the particular case of 'Socrates is wise,' and recall that the predicate in it is incomplete in being inseparable from that proposition and from the name 'Socrates': under no circumstances could it ever be placed between quotation marks. It is not a linguistic entity in its own right but is parasitic on expressions that genuinely are linguistic entities in their own right. It is of its essence to be *of* such complete entities.

Mutatis mutandis, therefore, exactly the same can be said of the incompleteness of the property to which the predicate refers, namely, Socrates' property of being wise. We can say that it is inseparable from Socrates—unlike what is claimed for the entities that tropes purport to be. Under no circumstances can it even be conceived of in isolation from Socrates, though of course the *universal* property of wisdom most certainly can be so conceived. It is of the essence of Socrates' wisdom that it be *of* him and not of any other individual. As such, it is of course not a universal property but an *instance* of that property.

An Objection to Predicate Instances

Since the notion of a property instance turns on the notion of a predicate instance, it might well be objected that this is an explanation of the obscure by the more obscure, for what possible sense could be made of predicate instances? A putative objection to predicate instances goes thus:

- In 'Socrates is wise' and 'Aristotle is wise' precisely the same is said of Socrates as is said of Aristotle.
- But, what is said of Socrates is the predicate instance in 'Socrates is wise' and what is said of Aristotle is the predicate instance in 'Aristotle is wise.'
- But, the predicate instances are not the same: they are distinct from each other, as well as not being interchangeable with each other.
- Therefore what is said of Socrates is *not* the same as what is said of Aristotle.
- Having agreed that what is said of Socrates *is* the same as what is said of Aristotle, the advocate of predicate instances seems compelled to accept that it is *not* the same after all.

- Since the notion of a predicate instance has contradictory entailments, there can be no such logical item as predicate instances.

The alleged contradiction could be sustained, however, only if what is said of Socrates and Aristotle were to be the same and not the same under precisely the same respect. Bearing that in mind, let us recall just how the two predicate instances do differ. Certainly, it is not that Aristotle is being said to be wise, whereas Socrates is being said to be only very nearly wise: each is said to be unqualifiedly wise. The difference between them is that one instance of the predicate can occur only in 'Aristotle is wise,' whereas the other can occur only in 'Socrates is wise.' The question at issue, therefore, is whether the predicable indicated by '___ can occur only in "Socrates (Aristotle) is wise"' says anything about Socrates (Aristotle). Obviously, it could do so only if it were a first-level predicate. So, the question is whether it really is a first-level predicate. If it were, then our two propositions should be elliptical for:

'Socrates is wise & can occur only in "Socrates is wise".'
'Aristotle is wise & can occur only in "Aristotle is wise".'

If that really were the case, there could be no denying that different things were indeed being said about Socrates and Aristotle. Clearly, that is not the case. The predicate indicated by '___ can occur only in "Socrates (Aristotle) is wise"' is being said neither of Socrates, nor Aristotle, nor of any other individual. Rather, it is being said of a predicable, namely, the predicable indicated by '___ is wise.' In other words, it is a metalinguistic predicate. Once that is recognized, there is little difficulty in answering the earlier objection. To have been effective, it had to show that acceptance of predicate instances entailed that what was said of Socrates was both the same and not the same as what was said of Aristotle. As it has now emerged, however, that claim is untenable.

The truth is that precisely the same first-level predicate is said of Socrates as is said of Aristotle. The difference between the instances of that predicate is one not of first-level predicates but of metalinguistic predicates. What is attributed to Socrates is neither more nor less than what is said of Aristotle. The difference is concerned solely with what is predicable of the *predicate instances* that are said of Socrates and Aristotle respectively. One instance is said to be able to occur only in 'Socrates is wise,' the other is said to be able to occur only in 'Aristotle is wise.' Consequently, although the predicate instances are admittedly both the same and not the same, they are the same under one respect and different under quite another. Contrary to the first objection, therefore, acceptance of predicate instances carries no commitment to any contradiction. Hence, given that ontological categories are to be determined by logical categories, one of which is predicate instances, the conclusion to be drawn is that the ontological correlates of predicate instances are *property* instances. And, since what is attached to 'Socrates' in 'Socrates exists' is a predicate instance, what is attributed to Socrates by that proposition is a property instance.

Once property instances have been recognized, it follows that neither existence nor wisdom can strictly speaking be said to be instantiated *by* Socrates. Rather, they are instantiated *by* their respective instances, which in turn exist *in* or are individuated by Socrates.

To sum up. The raison d'être of the present chapter has been merely to provide the prolegomena to a discussion of the relation between Socrates and his instance of existence which is central to the next chapter. The very possibility of any discussion at all depended on existence being a real property, which it has now proved to be. In addition, we needed to know what kind of entity Socrates' existence was, for an account of how he would be related to a universal existence would differ vastly from one of how he related to an instance of that universal. It was therefore crucial to decide whether, when one spoke of *his* existence, one was speaking of a universal property or one of its instances. The answer to emerge from the present chapter was yes, Socrates' existence is a real property instance. We are now equipped to determine just how unique is the relation between Socrates and his instance of existence.

four

A Paradigm Shift in Thinking about Existence

To have shown existence to be a real property of individuals is ipso facto to have opened the way for two powerful arguments against that same conclusion. It has been a case of one step forward and what seem to be two substantial steps backwards. It has forced us to recognize that, in an existing Socrates, there are two distinct but inseparable elements, one being the Socrates element and the other the existential element—the instance of existence—without which Socrates would of course be quite bereft of actuality.[1] The upshot is that the Socrates element has emerged as having no actuality whatsoever in its own right. Therein, however, lies the difficulty, for surely there can be no instance of a property without there being something for it to be a property of. How, then, could an instance of existence be a property of Socrates if there is nothing actual for it to be a property of? This is far and away the most powerful objection to existence being a real property.

The less powerful of the difficulties is the familiar point raised by Hume, Kant, and their many disciples in contending that Socrates' instance of existence could be a real property only if it added some-

---

1. Unlike David Lewis on the one hand and Alvin Plantinga on the other, I treat 'existence' and 'actuality' as synonyms. Similarly, I treat 'is actual' as a synonym for 'exists.'

thing to him. The clear, and apparently reasonable, assumption is that if his instance of existence were to be a real property, it should be like his other real but accidental property instances such as his wisdom. Since all of these undoubtedly do add something to him, his instance of existence should either do the same or forfeit all claim to being a real property. Although this contention has long cried out for an answer, I doubt that any have ever been satisfactory.

Before proceeding any further, however, it might be helpful to outline the strategy to be employed in addressing the two problems. The immediate task will be to determine whether an instance of existence is to be treated as at all special among Socrates' real properties. Does it conform to the same model as such a prototypical property as his wisdom? If not, just what is its distinguishing mark?

It will emerge that, whereas all other real properties are logically posterior to an individual in respect of actuality, an instance of existence is logically *prior* to an individual in respect of actuality. On the face of it such a relationship would seem to be impossible. It is impossible, however, only so long as we remain under the spell of the paradigm according to which a property instance has necessarily to *inhere* in the individual that has it. Only if that paradigm is loosened significantly can the problem be resolved. Section II in this chapter will therefore be devoted to showing that, in the case of existence, such a paradigm shift is indeed possible, a shift which removes any temptation to think of instances of existence as being required to *inhere* in individuals in order to qualify as property instances. That shift will be from requiring it to inhere in him to recognizing its being bounded by him.

The fruits of this shift will become evident in section III. It will be shown to entail that Socrates' instance of existence is not merely that by virtue of which he is something rather than nothing, but is also that by virtue of which he is a man, is wise, is intelligent, and so on. Importantly, it will also entail that it makes no sense to ask the question with which this chapter began, namely, what his existence 'adds' to him. Nor does it make any sense to ask what he 'subtracts' from existence. One implication of section IV, therefore, is that Hume and Kant were asking the wrong question.

Finally, a rebuttal will be needed against charges that a Socrates who is logically posterior to his existence in respect of actuality would surely have to be a property rather than a substance and, likewise, that his instance of existence would surely have to be a substance rather than a property instance. Section V will show that each of the charges rests on a non sequitur.

I. THE DISTINGUISHING MARK OF AN
INSTANCE OF EXISTENCE

First let me explain an item of terminology that I shall be using in this and following chapters:

- Instead of the long-winded 'Socrates is logically *prior* to his wisdom in respect of actuality,' I shall be saying that Socrates is the 'subject' of his instance of wisdom.[2]

---

2. As I shall be speaking often of logical priority and posteriority in the following pages, I should note that they have of course to be distinguished sharply from temporal priority and posteriority, not to mention from mathematical (as in a series) and spatial (as in a queue). To say that Socrates' instance of existence is logically prior to Socrates in respect of actuality is not at all to say that the former precedes the latter temporally. On the contrary, they are contemporaneous: independently of Socrates existing, there is neither the Socrates element nor his instance of existence. In the whole that is the existing Socrates there are two distinct but inseparable elements—Socrates and his existence. Each has a role, individuating in the case of Socrates and actualizing in the case of his instance of existence. To say that Socrates is logically prior to his instance of existence in respect of individuation is merely to draw attention to the fact that the individuating role belongs to Socrates, not to his instance of existence. It is certainly not to imply that Socrates has any kind of actuality *temporally* prior to exercising the individuating role. Similarly, to say that Socrates' instance of existence is logically prior to Socrates in respect of actuality is simply to say that the actualizing role in the existing Socrates belongs to his existence, not to Socrates. It is by no means to suggest that his instance of existence is like a trope in being actual irrespective of whether there is any individual to which it might belong.

- Instead of 'his wisdom is logically *posterior* to Socrates in respect of individuation,' I shall be saying that his instance of wisdom 'inheres' in Socrates.[3]

I might note that, besides being abbreviations, these locutions are metaphorical as well. Inevitably, therefore, they carry some misleading connotations against which we have always to be on our guard.[4]

Now, Socrates' instance of existence is clearly like his wisdom in being individuated by him. Obviously, however, it would make no sense to speak of an instance of wisdom as *inhering* in a subject, unless there were a subject in which to inhere—unless the subject had some actuality logically prior to the instance of wisdom that inheres in it. Hence, if Socrates' instance of *existence* were to inhere in him, it could do so only if there were a sense in which he had at least some minimal actuality even logically prior to his existing—even if it were no more than the *esse essentiae* espoused by Avicenna. Whether Socrates really does have such actuality depends on whether 'exists' would be predicable either of him or of some surrogate of him before his conception. Now, since friends of Propositions may be inclined to think that 'exists' certainly would be predicable of one or the other before Socrates' conception, we can proceed no further until their claim has been tested.

First, therefore, recall the distinction, due to Geach, between propositions and Propositions, which I mentioned in chapter 1. The point is that, whereas propositions are concrete, linguistic, and temporal, Propositions are abstract, non-linguistic, and atemporal. Notwithstanding that difference, Propositions are said to capture the thought expressed in propositions, but to capture it in non-linguistic form. It is also claimed that there could have been Propositions about Socrates even before he existed.

---

3. Although 'subject' and 'inheres' are Aristotelian terms, I intend them to be understood solely in the way I have outlined in this paragraph. If that coincides with Aristotle's sense, well and good; if not, it is of no consequence so far as this book is concerned.

4. For example, one might be tempted to conceive as 'inheres in a subject' after the manner of 'pins in a pin-cushion.'

Being abstract, Propositions could not of course include anything *non*-abstract like the term 'Socrates' or indeed any other *linguistic* component. Nevertheless, the Proposition which at some moment of time would come to be expressed linguistically as 'Socrates exists' would in fact have existed eternally, even though that linguistic expression of it would not. Whether it was true eternally, as some would contend, or varied in truth-value over time, as others think, is irrelevant for present purposes. The salient points about this proposal are that there would have been such a Proposition, and that this would have been the case even before Socrates' conception. It has to be noted, however, that the Proposition would not have been *directly* about Socrates, but only about something abstract that was intimately related to him, namely, a haecceity—a singular property that, *if* exemplified, could be exemplified only in Socrates. We might call it 'socrateity.'

On this hypothesis, then, long before Socrates' conception there would have been a Proposition that was about socrateity and was exemplifiable subsequently as 'Socrates exists.' Even if that were true, however, it would provide simply no answer at all to whether 'exists' could be predicated of *Socrates* before he existed. I make that claim because the issue is not whether there was any Proposition about socrateity, nor even whether that Proposition was exemplifiable by 'Socrates exists.' Rather, the point at issue is precisely *when* the Proposition could have been exemplified as 'Socrates exists,' and hence *when* 'exists' could have been predicated of Socrates. Could *that* have occurred before Socrates existed? If 'exists' were indeed predicable of Socrates at that time, Socrates must already have had some actuality either then or earlier.

Now, it might be claimed that, although the Proposition was not about Socrates, it was undoubtedly about socrateity. Would this not satisfy the test that 'exists' be predicable of either Socrates or his surrogate before his conception? Not really, for the surrogate being proposed is socrateity, which of course is an abstract entity. Unfortunately, although abstract entities can certainly be said to exist in some way or other, the term 'exists' can be used of such entities only in the *second*-level sense, but never in its first-level sense which is the only one of present concern.

To appreciate that point we need to distinguish very sharply indeed between the following claims:

- It is *always* the case that (a Proposition about socrateity is exemplifiable as 'Socrates exists').
- A Proposition about socrateity is *always* exemplifiable as 'Socrates exists.'

Although the first might be acceptable, it is irrelevant to our present concerns, for it allows of 'exists' (second-level) being predicated of the abstract entity *socrateity,* but sheds no light at all on whether 'exists' (*first*-level) could be predicated of the concrete entity *Socrates* before his conception. The only claim relevant to our concerns is the second, for it implies that at any time—even before Socrates' conception—the Proposition could have been exemplified as 'Socrates exists.' If so, then 'exists' would certainly have been predicable of Socrates before he existed.

The truth of that implication, however, is quite another matter, and cannot be established purely at the level of Propositions. Rather, it can be established only at the level of what Propositions can exemplify, which is at the level not of abstract entities (Propositions, haecceities) but of linguistic entities (propositions, proper names, and predicates). It is only at that linguistic level that we can establish whether the proposition 'Socrates exists' would have been possible before Socrates' conception. The argument, therefore, must now move from the abstract level—the level of Propositions—to the concrete level of language.

Was the proposition 'Socrates exists' possible before Socrates' conception?

In outline, the argument to show that there could have been no such proposition as 'Socrates exists' before Socrates' conception can be stated very simply. It turns on the uncontroversial claim that the possibility of a proposition 'Socrates exists' at any given time depends on whether 'Socrates' refers to Socrates at that time, i.e., whether

'"Socrates" refers to Socrates' is true at that time. Hence, 'Socrates exists' could have been a proposition before Socrates existed only if '"Socrates" refers to Socrates' could have been true at that time. Now, the argument against its being true at that time is one that relies on the simple truth that, once a proposition like '"Socrates" refers to Socrates' was true at a given time *a,* nothing *thereafter* could prevent its having been true at *a,* not even the death of Socrates. Incidentally, this point has sharply to be distinguished from the quite different claim that '"Socrates" refers to Socrates' could not be true at one time but false at a later time.

The argument goes as follows:

4.1. Had '"Socrates" refers to Socrates' been true at any time *a* before Socrates existed, it could *thereafter* never fail to have been true at time *a.*

4.2. But, until Socrates did come to exist it was *always* possible that he not come to exist, and hence that '"Socrates" refers to Socrates' should never have been true at time *a.*

4.3 Therefore, it is not the case that '"Socrates" refers to Socrates' could have been true at any time *a* before Socrates existed.

In arguing for the two premisses, it will be helpful to employ the following symbols:

Let *p* be the proposition '"Socrates" refers to Socrates.'
Let *a* be a time *before* Socrates came to exist.
Let *b* be any time *after a* but, nevertheless, still *before* Socrates came to exist.
Let 'T*ap*' be '*p* is true at time *a.*'
Let M be the operator 'it is possible that.'

Argument for Premiss (4.1):

4.4 Suppose that '"Socrates" refers to Socrates' had in fact been true at time *a* before he came to exist in 470 B.C., i.e.,T*ap.*

4.5. But, if that had been the case, then at time b it would have been no longer possible to prevent '"Socrates" refers to Socrates' from having been true at time a, i.e., Tap.

4.6 Therefore, at time b it would have been no longer possible to prevent '"Socrates" refers to Socrates' from having been true at time a, i.e., Tb~M~Tap.

4.7. But (4.6) entails that at time b it would not have been true that '"Socrates" refers to Socrates' possibly be prevented from having been true at a, i.e., ~TbM~Tap.

4.8. Therefore, at time b it would *not* have been true that '"Socrates" refers to Socrates' possibly be prevented from having been true at a, i.e., ~TbM~Tap.

Argument for Premiss (4.2):

4.9. It is possible that the conditions at time b could have been such as to have prevented Socrates from ever coming to exist.

4.10. But, had Socrates never come to exist, he could never have been referred to.

4.11. Therefore, at time b it would have been possible that 'Socrates' never have referred to Socrates.

4.12. But, had 'Socrates' *never* have referred to Socrates, '"Socrates" refers to Socrates' would not have been true at time a.

4.13. Therefore, at time b it *would* have been true that '"Socrates" refers to Socrates' possibly be prevented from having been true at a, i.e., TbM~Tap, which contradicts (4.8).

As for the source of the contradiction between (4.8) and (4.13), it is obvious that (4.8) is true if (4.5) is true, and that (4.13) is true if (4.9) is true. If both (4.5) and (4.9) are true, the contradiction will stem from the falsity of (4.4), namely, in supposing that '"Socrates" refers to Socrates' could have been true even before his conception. The argument turns, therefore, on (4.5) and (4.9), both of which will now bear closer attention.

Premiss (4.5): If '"Socrates" refers to Socrates' had in fact been true at time *a*, then at time *b* it would have been no longer possible to prevent '"Socrates" refers to Socrates' from having been true at time *a,* i.e., if T*ap* then T*b*~M~T*ap*.

This premiss claims merely that, *if* the proposition had been true at *a,* nothing *subsequent* to *a* could *then* have brought it about that the proposition *not* have been true at *a.* This is simply the unexceptional claim that the proposition could not have been both true and not true at the same time, namely, *a.* Hence, premiss (4.5) does not claim that, *if* '"Socrates" refers to Socrates' had been true at time *a,* it had *necessarily* to have been true at *a.* On the contrary, it allows that it might well not have been true at *a,* though such a possibility would have obtained only in the period *prior* to *a.* It is only subsequent to that time that there ceased to be any such possibility. The point is that, had it been a settled fact that '"Socrates" refers to Socrates' was indeed true at time *a,* nothing occurring subsequent to *a* could prevent its having been true at *a.* As Prior expressed it, 'the passage of time may eliminate "possibilities" in the sense of alternative outcomes of actual states of affairs, and cause that to be no longer alterable which once might have been otherwise.'[5]

Lest there be any suggestion of fatalistic implications in this premiss, consider that, according to fatalism, it is a logical or conceptual truth

> 4.14. that, if some particular state of affairs does *now* obtain or *has* obtained, then there was never any possibility either of its not obtaining or of its not having obtained, and
> 4.15. if some particular state of affairs *will* obtain, there is no possibility that it will not obtain.

Now, premiss (4.5) does not imply (4.14), since it does not claim that there would *never* have been any alternative to 'Socrates' referring to Socrates at time *a.* Rather, it claims merely that *subsequent* to that state of affairs obtaining at time *a,* there was *then* no possibility of

---

5. A. N. Prior, *Papers on Time and Tense* (Oxford: Oxford University Press, 1968), 77.

its not having obtained at time *a*. Nor is (4.15) implied, for premiss (4.5) is concerned solely with what *has* obtained, and has no implications at all for what has not yet obtained but *will* obtain. For these reasons, therefore, the premiss offers no support to fatalism.

Premiss (4.9): It is possible that conditions at time *b* could have been such as to have prevented Socrates from ever coming to exist.

This premiss would doubtless be strongly resisted by anyone of determinist bent. Such a one might insist that, before an individual existed, predictions could be made not simply about *some* individual or other, but about that very individual which does now exist. That is, such predictions could be singular rather than merely particular. Indeed, on this view, it might be argued that, even in 472 B.C., Socrates could have been referred to in terms of a then existing parcel of matter from which he could not have been prevented from coming to exist in 470 B.C.

Against this suggestion it must be said that Socrates' birth would have been unpreventable in 472 B.C. only under the following conditions, neither of which can be met:

4.16   If the universe were inherently deterministic in character.
4.17   If it were impossible that Socrates should have developed from energy or matter which, *subsequent to the prediction,* appeared in the universe from no prior source of energy or matter, e.g., if continuous or even discontinuous creation happened to occur in the universe subsequent to the prediction.

As for (4.16), the determinist view of nature would seem to be doubly confounded—on the one hand in the area of quantum mechanics, and on the other in the area of thermodynamics. Indeed, quantum mechanics threatens it in two ways. One is the ineradicably *statistical* character of quantum mechanical laws; the other is the *non-causal* character of those laws. Their statistical character alone makes it impossible to be specific about just what would follow upon any quantum mechanical event. Nor could this lack of specificity be dismissed as simply a defect afflicting our *knowledge,* but not at all reflected in the nature of things. On the contrary, the 'no hidden variable' argument has shown that the statistical character of the laws manifests an indeterminancy inherent in the universe and not eradicable even in principle by the supposition of hidden variables.[6] Hence, even if the laws had been causal, their causality would have been merely *probabilistic;* and even that suffices to undermine determinism. In fact, however, the laws are not causal at all, for it follows from the Bell Inequality[7] that quantum mechanics contains law-governed statistical correlations that bear *no causal* relation whatever to any earlier correlation. Not only are the later events not determinate effects of the earlier ones, they are not even *probabilistic* effects of earlier ones. That is one more reason for rejecting a deterministic universe.

In itself, the non-causal character of the laws should occasion no surprise, since we are already familiar with laws of just that kind, e.g., the Conservation Laws. Forrest calls them *negative* laws.[8] As distinct from *positive* laws, which tell us what does or is likely to cause what, negative laws tell us nothing of the sort. On the contrary, they tell us merely the *constraints* that are placed on a system, the limited possibilities available within a system. Although different from either the causal or the historical models of explanation, they are genuinely explanatory nevertheless, their explanatory role being to show that fewer possibilities are available than we may have thought.

As I said, there is nothing remarkable about negative laws *in se.* Nor would it be at all remarkable in the present instance for *some* of the laws in quantum mechanics to be negative ones. What does make it quite remarkable, however, is that *all* of them are negative laws: not one of them is causal.[9] *Without causality, however, there can be no determinism.* Nevertheless, there is nothing philosophically out-

---

6. S. Kochen and E. F. Specker, 'The Problem of Hidden Variables in Quantum Mechanics,' *Journal of Mathematics and Mechanics* 17 (1967): 59–87; G. Hellman, 'Einstein and Bell: Strengthening the Case of Microphysical Randomness,' *Synthese* 53 (1982): 461–504.

7. J. S. Bell, 'On the Einstein Podolsky Rosen Paradox,' *Physics* (1964): 106–200.

8. P. Forrest, *Quantum Metaphysics* (Oxford: Oxford University Press, 1988), 97.

9. Ibid., 144.

rageous about this absence of causality for there is no justification for insisting that the laws of nature be positive. Perhaps we have a metaphysical intuition that every change has a cause. But to convert that into an a priori argument for positive laws would require an extra premiss, namely that the physical sciences will serve to specify what causes what. And to assume that extra premiss a priori is, as Forrest says, to play Science Says.[10]

Thermodynamics presents itself as no less inimical to determinism than does quantum mechanics, and notably in regard to the behavior of a system when forced into a far-from-equilibrium condition that threatens its structure. Under those conditions it approaches a critical moment—a bifurcation point—at which Prigogine has concluded that it is *inherently* impossible to predict the next state of the system: its future course is purely a matter of chance. Once the new course is embarked upon, determinism takes over again until the next bifurcation point is reached. Moreover, the role of chance is not restricted simply to *what* happens at the bifurcation point, but extends also to the question of just *when* that point will occur: that, too, is unpredicable, even in principle.[11] So much, then, for condition (4.16). Of the findings of thermodynamics and those of quantum mechanics, *either* would have sufficed to show that the universe was not inherently determinist. As it happens, both do.

As for (4.17), the creation of matter or energy would be untenable on intrinsic grounds only if every change were to require a cause. As we have just seen, however, even at the macro level not all laws are causal, and at the level of quantum mechanics no law is causal. Consequently, not every change requires a cause; and that means that the coming to be of energy or matter from no prior source within the universe remains intrinsically possible—not only logically possible but physically possible as well. Indeed, it is a respectable notion in science, having already been employed in cosmological theory by Hoyle and abandoned by him, not because of any problem inherent

---

10. Ibid., 44–45.

11. I. Prigogine and I. Stengers, *Order out of Chaos: Man's New Dialogue with Nature* (New York: Bantam, 1964).

in the notion, but simply because the evidence seemed to support a different hypothesis to account for the state of the universe.

Not only can the possible creation of matter not be precluded on intrinsic grounds, it cannot be precluded on extrinsic grounds either, since no state of affairs could preclude the creation of matter unless that event were dependent on already existing matter. There could be no such dependence, however, for the creation of matter is *ex hypothesi* the coming to be of matter or energy from *no* prior matter or energy. For these reasons, therefore, it is not impossible that Socrates should have developed from energy or matter which appeared from no prior matter or energy and which could not have been referred to at the time of the prediction, since at that time it would neither have existed nor have been able to be predicted. Thus, condition (4.17) is no more satisfied than is condition (4.16), and that removes the challenge to (4.9). Moreover, since both (4.5) and (4.9) have now been vindicated, we are left with the conclusion that Socrates could not have been referred to before his conception.

A point to bear in mind when considering the argument is that the necessity being employed in it is not logical, but is the kind which Prior confessed to borrowing from Ferdinand of Cordova, namely, the notion of a truth that can no longer be prevented because the time for preventing it is now past.[12] Consequently, I am not saying it would have been *logically* impossible at b that '"Socrates" refers to Socrates' not have been true at a. I am saying simply that at b it was no longer possible to *prevent* '"Socrates" refers to Socrates' from having being true at a.

The same point can be expressed by paraphrasing Gilbert Ryle to the effect that the prediction of the birth of a son to the man and woman who came later to generate Socrates could, in principle, be as specific as you please. But one thing the forecaster could not do— logically and not merely epistemologically could not do. In his prediction he could not use with their normal force the term 'Socrates' or the pronoun 'he.'[13] At no time before Socrates' conception could

---

12. A. N. Prior, *Papers on Time and Tense*, 76.

13. G. Ryle, *Dilemmas* (Cambridge: Cambridge University Press, 1954), 27.

'Socrates' have referred to him. As Prior once intimated, not even God could do that.[14]

Before leaving this section it is worth recalling just what was the point of arguing that Socrates could not be referred to before his conception.

- The point was to show that there is no truth to the proposal that 'A Proposition about socrateity is always exemplifiable as "Socrates exists,"'[15] a claim that friends of Propositions might have been inclined to endorse.
- And the whole point of *that* lengthy exercise was to show that, before Socrates' conception, there was nothing in which his instance of existence or any other property could possibly inhere.
- That is to say, his existence could not be logically posterior to him in respect of actuality.
- And that conclusion was designed to highlight the crucial difference between two kinds of Socrates' real properties—between his existence on the one hand and all his other real properties on the other. The latter are logically posterior to (parasitic upon) an individual in respect of actuality. The former, however, is not. Rather, it is ontologically prior to an individual in respect of actuality. That is, the metaphor of 'inherence' is simply not applicable to it. What, then, could a correlative metaphor be? If inherence is not a possible metaphor for the role of existence, just what is?

II. A New Paradigm

Before seeking to establish the appropriate metaphor for the role of existence, it may be helpful first to list some of the more general conclusions reached so far about first-level properties.

---

14. A. N. Prior, 'Identifiable Individuals' in his *Papers on Time and Tense*, 72.

15. The falsity of that de re proposition is of course quite consistent with the truth of the correlative de dicto proposition, 'It is always the case that (a Proposition about socrateity is exemplifiable as "Socrates exists").'

- A first-level property is *whatever can be attributed to an individual by a predicate.*
  Note that this definition uses the term 'attributed' rather than 'added.' Whether everything attributed to an individual is also 'added' to it is a further question.
- First-level properties may be relational or non-relational.
- Some relational ones are Cambridge, others real. Non-relational ones are real.
- Real first-level properties may be logically prior to an individual with respect to actuality, or they may be logically posterior to it.
- Existence is logically prior to an individual, all other real properties are logically posterior.
- If logically *posterior,* they add something to an individual. Whether this is true of a property that is logically *prior* is, however, a question to be addressed in section IV of this chapter.
- A common metaphor applicable to logically posterior properties is that they 'inhere' in an individual.
- As was established in the previous section, however, it is just that metaphor of inherence which is quite inapplicable to existence, precisely because existence is logically prior to an individual in respect to actuality.

The foregoing points may be schematized as shown in figure 4.1.

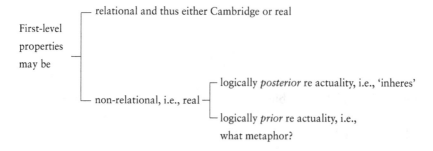

The last of these points highlights our lack of a metaphor that would do for the role of existence what 'inheres' does for the role of an instance of wisdom. Until that lack has been made good, however, the full import of the difference between logical posteriority and logical priority to an individual in respect of actuality is less likely to strike home. Expressed metaphorically, 'An instance of wisdom is logically posterior to an individual in respect of actuality' becomes 'An instance of wisdom inheres in an individual.' What is the corresponding metaphorical expression of 'An instance of existence is logically prior to an individual in respect of actuality'? Is there one, or perhaps more than one, metaphor that will so contrast with 'inheres' as to give striking expression to the difference between logical posteriority and logical priority in respect of actuality?

A Possible Metaphor

A clue to such a metaphor is offered by the homely analogy of a block of butter that has been cut into a number of parts. Each piece of butter has a different surface or bound. A peculiar thing about bounds is that, although they are real enough, they themselves are totally devoid of thickness: they are not to be mistaken for an enveloping film whether of butter or of any other material whatsoever. Despite their ontological poverty, however, they do have a genuine function, for they serve to distinguish every block from every other block. In that sense they can be said to individuate the blocks they bound.

If one is asked how something that is totally devoid of matter can have this distinguishing role, the answer is simply 'That is just what it means to be a bound rather than, say, a container.' Bounds individuate what they bound, but containers presuppose that their contents are already individuated. Now, our question about Socrates is, 'What kind of metaphor would be applicable to Socrates being logically posterior to his existence in respect of actuality?' 'Inheres' is an appropriate metaphor for the way in which Socrates' wisdom relates to him, but what would be a corresponding metaphor for the way in which his existence does so? The butter analogy strongly suggests the metaphor of 'bounded by'—Socrates' instance of wisdom 'inheres' in him, his instance of existence is 'bounded by' him. While accepting 'inheres' and 'bounded by' as suitable metaphors, I do not preclude the possibility of there being others perhaps equally suitable. Although it is true that all first-level properties are locked into being either logically prior or logically posterior to individuals in respect of actuality, it may not be true that they are locked into having no more than two corresponding metaphors. 'Bounded by' or 'bound' is therefore the metaphor that I shall adopt.

I should note that, just as 'inheres' adds nothing of substance to the fact that Socrates is logically prior to his instance of wisdom in respect of actuality, so 'bounded by' adds nothing of substance to the fact that Socrates is logically posterior to his instance existence. Rather than adding anything of substance, each of them supplies a convenient metaphor for expressing more vividly what 'logically prior in respect of actuality' and 'logically posterior in respect of actuality' express more prosaically. Let it not be thought, however, that either metaphor is absolutely essential to any discussion of existence, for whatever conclusions can be drawn by using them could also be drawn—albeit not without prolixity and inelegance—by using the notions of logical priority or posteriority with respect to actuality.

Perhaps this has been too quick, so let me suggest another way of commending the metaphor 'bounds.'

- There are two elements in an existing Socrates. One is an instance of existence. The other is what is actualized by that instance of existence, namely, the Socrates element, including, of course, all his properties.
- Although the instance of existence exhausts all the actuality in the existing Socrates, the Socrates element is not superfluous.
- But if it is not superfluous, what possible role can it play?

The role of bounding (not of containing) the instance of existence would seem to be peculiarly appropriate, given that Socrates, considered in se, is entirely devoid of all actuality. This is consistent with the fact that, as the bound of his instance of existence, Socrates would ipso facto be its individuator as well. It is also consistent with his instance of existence being his actualizer, that by virtue of which he is something rather than nothing.[16] Moreover, with Socrates understood as the bound of his existence, there is no longer any difficulty in reconciling the following relations, the conjunction of which might otherwise have seemed so perplexing:

---

16. As will be evident in the following chapter, that is far from exhausting the role of his existence.

- In respect of actuality, Socrates is logically posterior to his instance of existence.
- In respect of individuation, Socrates is logically prior to his instance of existence.

Once Socrates is understood as bounding his instance of existence, there is no difficulty in understanding his being logically prior to it in respect of individuation but logically posterior to it in respect of actuality.

Putting it another way, the notion of Socrates as the bound of his instance of existence assists in resolving the following two puzzles that otherwise might have seemed insoluble.

- Socrates has no actuality in his own right. How, then, could his instance of existence be a property instance when there is nothing for it to be a property of?

or

- Socrates individuates his instance of existence. Just how is that possible, if he has no actuality in his own right?

Prior to this chapter, it may have been thought that whatever was attributable to an individual by a predicate was coextensive with whatever could inhere in an individual. The merit of the present section has been to stress how existence can be a property of individuals even though it does not inhere in them. Existence thus breaches the erstwhile paradigm for first-level properties, but qualifies perfectly well as a property nevertheless. It is as much a property as are those, like wisdom, that are typical of that paradigm.

III. Dual Role for Socrates

At first sight it might seem that the sole role of Socrates as bounding his instance of existence is to individuate it.[17] If that were true,

---

17. There is also a dual role for Socrates' *instance of existence*. Although it would not be entirely out of place to discuss it in the present chapter, it sits more comfortably in the following one, where the wealth of existence is the central topic.

however, his role vis-à-vis his existence would be no different from that of Gerard (a gnat) or any other individual. In remarking on Socrates' role as a bound, therefore, it would be a grave oversight not to recognize that Socrates has a further role. I refer to the fact that, in bounding his existence, he provides a pattern of the various limits to which that actuality extends, namely, his intelligence, his wisdom, his generosity, and so on. This role might be described as one of 'socratizing' his instance of existence. Obviously, since Socrates is a far more complex individual than a gnat or a grain of sand, the limits on the reach of his existence constitute a correspondingly more complex pattern or bound than theirs.[18]

The notion of Socrates and his existence which has now emerged is one that depicts Socrates as having a dual role vis-à-vis his instance of existence. One is as individuating it, which is precisely the roles that Plato and Aristotle have vis-à-vis their respective instances of existence, constituting the numerical difference between them. The other role, as has just been noted, is that of socratizing his instance of existence. Although that may seem a strange—even preposterous— claim, it is nothing more than a shorthand way of noting that Socrates is the mark on his instance of existence of a very complex pattern of limits, a pattern whose role is analogous—but only analogous— to the way a plan marks the structure of a building or a blueprint marks the structure of an electrical circuit. The bound which is the Socrates element maps the reaches of his instance of existence.

Besides marking its numerical difference from other instances of existence, the bound which is the Socrates element has therefore the further role of marking its qualitative differences and similarities as well. There is nothing esoteric about this claim, for it follows immediately from the very simple fact that the reaches of his instance of existence can be neither more nor less than the limits that are the mark of the Socrates element.

---

18. Socrates is not simply a pattern, however, but an *individuated* one. Although the numerically one pattern cannot occur in any existing individual but Socrates, there is of course no obstacle to its being cloned. The relation between clones is a far cry from one of identity.

A very rough analogy might be offered by a light beam set behind a glass screen bearing the hues and patterns of a Monet painting. When the light shines through it, the screen might be said to 'Monetize' the light, to put its stamp on it, a stamp that would be incomparably more complex than, say, that produced by a glass screen that was merely half red and half blue. The Monet screen is analogous to the Socrates element as marking the limits of his instance of existence, the light beam is analogous to Socrates' instance of existence, and the red and blue screen is analogous to, say, a grain of sand as bound of its existence.[19] This example may assist in understanding what is meant by saying that, in bounding his instance of existence, Socrates 'socratizes' it.[20]

In summary, then, the following points are critical to understanding what it means to say that the Socrates element is the bound of his existence:

- The Socrates element has no actuality independently of his instance of existence. Thus, it ought not be conceived of as a kind of outer layer on that instance, and still less as a kind of container. Both conceptions would entail its having some actuality in its own right—independently of its instance of existence.
- Its sole role is in being a map of the reaches of its instance of existence. It itself does not actively set or impose bounds or limits, but merely is those bounds or limits.
- This pattern or imprint, which is the Socrates element, is individuated not by any individuator, but in its own right.

---

19. Naturally, the analogy limps, for the light beam is an entity in its own right, which Socrates' instance of existence most certainly is not. Moreover, the light beam can extend beyond the glass screen, whereas it makes no sense to say that the instance of existence could extend the bounds marked by the Socrates element. Moreover again, even the glass screen has some actuality in its own right, which Socrates (considered independently of his instance of existence) certainly does not.

20. Remember that Socrates, Plato, and Aristotle do not *operate* on their instances of existence in any way. The role of individuals is not to *do* something to their instances of existence, but simply to *be* something to them, namely, the bounds or imprints on them.

- Finally, although I have sometimes spoken only of Socrates as the bound of his instance of existence, strictly speaking it is Socrates with all his nonexistential properties that is the bound. This should have been obvious enough, since the properties have no more actuality independently of the instance of existence than does Socrates himself.

Here is another analogy. If readers find it more of a hindrance than a help, they should try to ignore it. Consider now a glass sphere with an etching on its surface. Let the surface be analogous to an individual, and the glass of the sphere be analogous to an individual's instance of existence. Compare, then, the items in the columns below.

Sphere with minimal etching	Simplest existing individual
Sphere with more complex etching	Second simplest existing individual
Sphere with still more complex etching	Third simplest existing individual
. .	. .
. .	. .
Sphere with yet more complex etching	Complex individual—chimpanzee
Sphere with yet more complex etching	More complex individual—human

Now notice the following parallels:

- The surface contributes no glass to the sphere.
  The individual element (e.g., the Socrates element) in an existing individual contributes nothing by way of actuality.
- The etching on the sphere may vary from the simplest to the most complex.
  Individuals that bound their instance of existence are patterns of limits, and vary from the simplest to the most complex.
- Even the most complex etching contributes no glass to the sphere.
  Even the most complex of individuals contributes no actuality to its existence.

This analogy is intended to illustrate the point that, in conceiving of Socrates as the bound of his instance of existence, one needs to remember that, like the etched surface of the sphere, the role of the Socrates element is simply that of a pattern or imprint on his instance of existence, but not in any way that of an actualizer.

In conclusion, recall that the paradigm shift entailed by conceiving of Socrates as the bound of his existence has been impelled by the twin demands that his existence be a real property and that Socrates in se has no actuality for it to be a property of. In other words, the prima facie problem was how to reconcile his being logically prior to his instance of existence in respect of individuation, but logically posterior to it in respect of actuality. How could Socrates have any role at all relative to his instance of existence without having some actuality independently of it? In particular, how could he individuate his instance of existence without having some actuality independently of that instance? These bore the appearance of difficulties precisely because we were seduced by the metaphor of properties having to 'inhere' in an individual. They ceased being difficulties once it was recognized that an acceptable role for instances of existence was that of 'being bound by' an individual.[21] The distinction between individuating by being a bound and individuating by being a subject of inherence is an absolute one: 'is bounded by' is no less a primitive relational metaphor than is 'inheres in.'

---

21. Although some medieval writers spoke of Socrates as 'contracting' or 'determining' his existence, it is doubtful whether they regarded him as *bounding* it. Aquinas, for example, speaks of the existence of a created form as being 'received and contracted to a determinate nature' [receptum et contractum ad determinatam naturam]' (*Summa Theologica,* I, 7, 2c). Even more interesting is: 'In everything that exists subsequent to the first being, . . . its existence is received in something that contracts it' [Omne igitur quod est post primum ens, . . . habet esse in aliquo receptum, per quod ipsum esse contrahitur]' (*De Creaturis Spiritualibus,* 1c). This might seem to suggest that the contraction of existence was a consequence of its being *received* in Socrates. Confirming this interpretation is a passage in which, speaking of things that are inferior to subsistent existence, Aquinas remarks that they are things 'in which existence is not subsisting but *inhering*' [in quibus esse non est subsistens, sed inhaerens] (*De Potentia,* q.7, a.2. ad 7 um). As reflected in these texts, Aquinas would seem to regard existence as being received in an individual, as inhering in an individual. I have been arguing, on the contrary, that an instance of existence is neither, but is bounded by an individual.

IV. Does Existence Add Anything to Socrates?

I turn now to the second of the questions that precipitated this chapter, namely, 'What is added to Socrates by his instance of existence?' As I have remarked, great play has been made of questions like 'Just what is Socrates' instance of existence, if it is not Socrates, nor any of his (nonexistential) properties, whether relational or not? What difference does it make? Just what does it add to him?' Purporting to be purely rhetorical, such questions have sometimes been thought to deliver the coup de grâce to all possibility of existence being a real property of individuals. Hume dismissed it with his remark that the idea of existence 'when conjoined with the idea of an object makes no addition to it,'[22] and Kant did the same in observing that 'a hundred thalers do not contain the least coin more than a hundred possible thalers,'[23] a more contemporary variant of which is expressed by Paul Davies as 'I can meaningfully talk about having five little coins in my pocket, but what does it mean for me to say that I have five existing coins and six nonexistent coins?'[24]

Much the same point is made by those who are troubled by the fact that 'exists' is clearly not what they call a 'descriptive' predicate.[25] In 'Socrates exists,' the predicate is charged with telling us neither what kind of entity Socrates is, nor what distinguishes him from any other individual. 'It would be senseless to suppose that an object may be singled out, whether in perception or imagination or thought, as having it [existence].'[26] Existence does not provide any basis for classifying an individual with other individuals nor for setting the one apart from the others. Saying that something exists, therefore, adds nothing to the concept of anything. Descriptive predicates do

---

22. D. Hume, *Treatise of Human Nature*.

23. I. Kant, *Critique of Pure Reason*, B627.

24. P. Davies, *The Mind of God* (New York: Simon and Schuster, 1992), 185.

25. E.g., M. Munitz, *Existence and Logic* (New York: New York University Press, 1974), 166–67.

26. P. Butchvarov, *Being qua Being* (Bloomington: Indiana University Press, 1979), 109.

these kinds of things, but the predicate 'exists' does none of them. Failure to be a descriptive predicate is thus presented as irrefutable evidence that 'exists' cannot be a real predicate.

Remarks like the foregoing may well have made very good sense had existence been a property like wisdom, which objectors seem tacitly to have assumed that any real property would have to resemble. Given that misconception, it might indeed have been argued that, since we can say what his instance of wisdom adds to Socrates, we should surely be no less forthcoming about what his instance of existence adds to him—if in fact it adds anything at all. It is, however, precisely because Socrates is logically prior to his instance of existence—a recipient or subject of his instance of wisdom—that 'What does his wisdom add to Socrates?' can quite reasonably be asked. Yet that question, which is entirely appropriate for any property instance of which Socrates is the recipient or subject of inherence, is quite inappropriate for a property instance—of existence—of which Socrates is certainly not its recipient but its bound.

The point is that a bound is not something to which anything at all can be 'added.' It makes as little sense to ask what an instance of existence adds to its bound (Socrates) as to ask what a sphere adds to its bound (its surface). So, the question 'What does his (instance of) existence add to Socrates?' is unanswerable not because the criticisms are well-founded, but because they are so desperately ill-founded, resting as they do on the misconception that Socrates' instance of existence could not be a real property unless it were like his instance of wisdom. And that particular delusion stems from the single-minded concentration on Socrates' existence as being a property instance and the correlative neglect of what is peculiar to it as being an *existential* property instance.

What, then, would the legitimate question be? I mentioned in note 21 that existence has sometimes been spoken of as 'contracted' by Socrates. Bearing that in mind, one might perhaps be tempted to think that the appropriate question would be not what his instance of existence adds to Socrates but what Socrates subtracts from existence as such. But underlying this question is exactly the same misconception as bedevilled the earlier one, for it too assumes that Socrates receives his instance of existence—is logically prior to it—

and thereby contracts it. The truth, therefore, is that it makes no more sense to ask what Socrates subtracts from his instance of existence than it does to ask what it adds to him.

The proper question is one which accepts the notion of a first-level property as 'whatever is attributable to an individual by a predicate,' but without presuming that attributing something to an individual is inseparable from adding something to it. Rather than ask 'What does his instance of existence add to Socrates?' therefore, the proper question would be 'What does his instance of existence attribute to Socrates?' The answer, of course, depends on how his instance of existence relates to Socrates. Had the relation been one of inherence, one might reasonably have expected that what was attributed to him would have constituted an addition to him. Given that the relation is one of being bounded, any such expectation would have been quite groundless. Rather than adding anything to the Socrates element, his instance of existence simply actualizes it and is socratized by it. And it makes no more sense to conceive of actualizing or being socratized as adding anything to him than to conceive of lifting a weight in the air as adding anything to it.

Incidentally, this happens to confirm the earlier conclusion, if any confirmation were necessary, that existence is a real property. I say that because Socrates himself could not be real unless what he bounds were also real. A bound cannot be more real than what it bounds.

V. Removing Ontological Misconceptions

The suggestion that the Socrates/instance-of-existence relation is one of bound to bounded might seem to be distinctly counter-intuitive, for surely we conceive of a property instance as belonging to Socrates, not of Socrates as belonging to a property instance. Yet, if the bound/bounded relation is to be taken seriously, surely the bound must belong to what it bounds, and Socrates might well seem to belong to his instance of existence rather than vice versa. Thus conceived of, his instance of existence would seem to be a substance or at least something very much like a substance. Socrates, who is indeed a prototypical substance, would therefore not be a substance after all.

These disconcerting considerations need to be addressed. Hence, before finally accepting that Socrates really is the bound of his instance of existence, the following questions need to be confronted.

- How can Socrates' role as a substance be reconciled with his being the bound of his instance of existence?
- How can the role of Socrates' instance of existence as a property instance be reconciled with its being bounded by Socrates?

Questions of this kind are not to be settled by appeals to such imaginative analogies as comparing properties to pins in a pin cushion or substance to a kernel in a nut, or even to rather more sophisticated pictorial representations. Exercises of imagination are inevitably misleading, since substance and property can only be conceived of, not pictured. They can no more be pictured than can black swans that are not black, four-dimensional space-time, the singularity espoused by the Big Bang theory, or wisdom as such, all of which—including black swans that are not black—are eminently conceivable.[27]

In trying to determine whether a Socrates that is the bound of his existence could be a substance, we should try to conceive of it at least by specifying the necessary and sufficient conditions for being a substance as well as those for being a property instance, namely:

- Primary substance: That it be concrete and individuated in se.[28]
- First-level property instance: That it be concrete and individuated not in se, but by the individual that has it.

---

27. Contradictions may be unimaginable, but nothing is simpler than to conceive of them, which is exactly what happens in reductio ad absurdum arguments. Again, it is impossible to imagine a nonexistent Socrates, but it can readily be conceived of, which is precisely what we do in grasping the proposition 'Socrates does not exist.' Dummett reminds us (*Frege, Philosophy of Language,* 473) that Frege, too, maintained that the self-contradictory could nevertheless be meaningful.

28. A concrete entity is any entity that is capable of causing change, or of undergoing change, or of both. On this criterion, such entities may be either material or immaterial, complete or incomplete, individuals or even property instances (though not universal properties). Dummett makes the

The questions then to be asked of Socrates and his existence are these:

- Does Socrates, conceived of as the bound of his instance of existence, satisfy the necessary and sufficient conditions for being a substance?
- Does Socrates' instance of existence, conceived of as being bounded by Socrates, satisfy the necessary and sufficient conditions for being a (first-level) property instance?

What about the first of these questions? Perhaps it would be objected that, if Socrates were a bound in the way I have claimed him to be, would he not be incapable of causing or undergoing any change? I reply that this charge could be sustained only if Socrates were considered in abstraction from his instance of existence. Considered in abstraction from it, however, he would be impotent to do or suffer anything at all, irrespective of how he were conceived of—whether as a bound, or as a subject of inherence, or in any other way. So that can hardly count as an objection to his being a bound. Socrates, conceived of not in abstraction from his instance of existence but as actually bounding it, would be capable of causing and suffering change when bounding his instance of existence, and hence would be a concrete entity.

As to whether the bound is individuated in se, the alternative would be that it be individuated ab alio, namely, by what it bounds. In the case of a glass sphere, for example, this is clearly not so. Its spatial bound could be individuated by the sphere only if the sphere were individuated without a bound—which is impossible. And, speaking generally, a bound can be said to be individuated in se, and not by what it bounds. Being individuated in se, therefore, Socrates qua bound satisfies also the second part of the necessary and sufficient condition for being a primary substance, an individual.

We might turn now to consider whether an instance of existence satisfies the necessary and sufficient condition for being a property instance. Clearly, if a bound is concrete, then the bounded can hardly

---

same general point more succinctly: 'a concrete entity can take part in causal interactions: an abstract object can neither cause nor be the subject of change' (*Frege, Philosophy of Language,* 91).

be abstract. Moreover, if the bound is individuated in se, the bounded must be individuated ab alio. Being bounded, therefore, does not disqualify Socrates' instance of existence from being a property instance. Thus, if we abjure imagination and consider only the necessary and sufficient conditions for being a primary substance and those for being a property instance had by a primary substance, the bound is not precluded from being a substance nor the bounded from being a property instance. In particular, the status of Socrates as a primary substance and of his instance of existence as a first-level property instance are quite compatible with their being related as bound to bounded. This may not satisfy our imagination, but why should it?

There is yet another difficulty for, although the general notion of substance is consistent with that of being a bound, it might be objected that the notion of a material substance most certainly is not. The difficulty is that a material substance is obviously a stuff, which is precisely what a bound is not. Seemingly, therefore, a material substance could hardly be a bound. Consequently, since Socrates is undoubtedly a material substance, he could not be the bound of his instance of existence.

This objection, too, represents a triumph of imagining over conceiving.[29] The fact is that the stuff in question is not Socrates qua [divorced from his instance of existence, but Socrates qua having] his

---

29. Theodore Scaltsas makes the same mistake in comparing existing with separateness. Speaking of the latter, he remarks that a test of its *not* being a property 'is that we *cannot abstract away separateness* from our representation of a substance.' He then adds, 'Ditto with "existing"' (T. Scaltsas, *Substance and Universals in Aristotle's Metaphysics* [Ithaca: Cornell University Press, 1994], 98. Emphasis in the original). In his view, therefore, existence is disqualified from being a property of Socrates simply because it cannot be abstracted from our *representation* (image) of him. This putative test is relevant, however, only to our ability to *imagine* Socrates without his existence, but quite irrelevant to our ability to *conceive* of him without it which, as I have said, is something we readily do in grasping propositions like 'Socrates does not exist.'

Yet another example of trying to imagine existence rather than to conceive of it would be to depict it, as did J. L. Austin, as 'something that things

instance of existence. To think that Socrates qua divorced from his instance of existence is a stuff is to regress to the already discredited notion of Socrates as having some actuality even logically prior to his instance of existence. Precisely because he is logically posterior to it in respect of actuality, however, it is quite impossible—logically impossible—that there be any Socrates independently of his instance of existence. In fact, Socrates as so conceived would be neither material nor immaterial, and hence the material/immaterial dichotomy would be no more appropriate to him than the shapely/unshapely dichotomy is appropriate to a twinge of pain. The material/immaterial distinction is appropriate only to Socrates qua existing; and it is only qua existing that Socrates can be said to be a stuff.[30]

VI. THE TWO CHALLENGES

The previous chapter concluded that Socrates' existence was an instance of a real property, not a Cambridge one. The present chapter has been responding to two challenges to that conclusion, each of them purporting to show that it could not possibly be true. The first appealed to the putative tautology that nothing could be a property of an individual unless there were an individual for it to be a property of. Surely an instance of existence could not be a real property of Socrates unless there were a Socrates for it to be a property instance of. But to say that the actuality of an existing Socrates is attributable solely to his instance of existence is ipso facto to say that Socrates is devoid of any actuality in his own right, and hence there is nothing for his instance of existence to be a property of. That would seem to preclude any suggestion that existence is a real property.

---

do all the time, like breathing, only quieter—ticking over, as it were, in a metaphysical sort of way' (J. L. Austin, *Sense and Sensibilia* [Oxford: Oxford University Press, 1962], 62).

30. Naturally, anyone who denied that existence was a real property would draw no distinction between Socrates qua divorced from his instance of existence and Socrates qua existing, and hence would have no difficulty in affirming unequivocally that Socrates was indeed a stuff.

The second challenge was less threatening, and relied on the claim that, if Socrates' instance of existence were indeed real, it should make some addition to him. After all, since every nonexistential real property does precisely that, why should existence not do so—if it truly were a real property? The question was, of course, intended to be purely rhetorical, and to compel the conclusion that existence was not a real property.

Each of the challenges would have precluded the reality of existence, had only their shared assumption been sound. The assumption was that an F could be a property of individual a only if it inhered in a, only if it were logically posterior to a in respect of actuality. The heart of the chapter lay in pinpointing the flaw in that assumption and the need to accept a paradigm shift from thinking that all first-level properties must inhere in an individual to recognizing that at least one property (existence) required only to be bounded by an individual. Being the bound of its instance of existence, an individual could hardly have been expected to have any actuality in its own right, nor could it have been expected to be logically posterior to its existence in respect of actuality. So, the first challenge, which had been presented as insuperable, proved not to be insuperable after all.

The second challenge, too, was flawed by the assumption that the sole way in which an F could be a property of a was for it to inhere in a, to be logically posterior to a in respect of actuality. Once the flaw in that presupposition had been exposed, it was not difficult to expose also the vanity of questions like 'What does his instance of existence add to Socrates?' Often regarded as purely rhetorical, they were revealed in their true hues—as simply a nonsense. They are a nonsense not because instances of existence are merely instances of a Cambridge property, as some might think, but because the notion of a property 'adding' anything to an individual is quite at odds with its being bounded by that individual. So much, then, for the second challenge.

With this defeat of the twin challenges, the last serious objection to an instance of existence being accepted as a real property of concrete individuals has proved to be utterly devoid of substance. Yet, there does remain a further question for, even if instances of existence are finally accepted as real properties, they might nevertheless be suspected of being the most impoverished of all property instances. Whether that charge can be sustained is for the following chapter to determine.

five

The Fecundity of the Paradigm Shift— The Wealth of Existence

The paradigm shift embraced in the previous chapter marked a critical advance in our understanding of existence as a real property of individuals. It did not, however, mark the end of the story. Rather, it has provided the basis upon which to respond to two further questions:

- How does an instance of existence rate ontologically vis-à-vis instances of *non*existential real properties? Is it ontologically richer? Or ontologically poorer?
- How do instances of existence rate ontologically vis-à-vis each other? Is Kenny right in thinking that the difference between them is no more than a numerical one?

These are questions that could not have arisen for Hume and Kant, since existence was no part of their ontology. Once existence is recognized as a real property, however, they are inescapable. They will be addressed in this chapter, which will witness to the fecundity of the paradigm shift in our thinking about existence.

I. ARGUMENTS FOR THE POVERTY OF EXISTENCE

An argument offered by Anthony Kenny appeals to the fact that existence is had by everything from the most fleeting of sub-atomic particles, to stones, to amoebae, to trees, to fish, to dogs, and to humans of all kinds ranging from the most severely brain damaged to Aristotle and Einstein. From this he concludes that '"to be" [understood as a very general, a very fundamental predicate] seems to be the thinnest possible kind of predicate; to be, so understood, is to have that attribute which is common to mice and men, dust and angels.'[1] Elsewhere he argues that if existence is an attribute which is possessed or an activity that is performed by anything which is anything, then 'exists' seems to be 'the totally uninformative highest [but minimal] common factor of all predicates.'[2] These claims are not totally implausible for, if existence is common to all such entities from the lowest to the highest, there is perhaps a prima facie puzzle as to how it could ever justly enjoy the elevated status that some have ascribed to it.

Christopher Hughes reached much the same conclusion, though by a rather different route. He did so in the course of contesting the claim that 'different sorts of *esses* will be limited to varying extents by different sorts of forms,'[3] a view expressed by Aquinas in saying that 'a thing is more or less excellent according as its *esse* is limited to a greater or lesser special mode of excellence.'[4] Hughes will have none of this. As he says, 'I think I can understand the difference between having whiteness according to its full power and having whiteness according to something less than its full power because, I take it, it is the difference between being less than perfectly white and being perfectly white. By contrast, there does not seem to be a difference between being perfectly existent and being less than perfectly existent.'[5] Existence, he contends, is therefore an 'on/off' property. His argument for its invariance is simply this.

> Existence is an on/off property: 'either you're there or you're not.' Because existence is on/off, it would seem, either you have it according to its full power or you don't have it at all.

1. A. Kenny, *The Five Ways* (London: Routledge and Kegan Paul, 1969), 92.

2. A. Kenny, *Aquinas* (Oxford: Oxford University Press, 1980), 57.

3. C. Hughes, *On a Complex Theory of a Simple God* (Ithaca: Cornell University Press, 1989), 26. Emphasis in the original.

4. Aquinas, *Summa contra Gentiles,* Book I, c.28.

5. C. Hughes, *A Complex Theory,* 27.

The inference to be drawn, thinks Hughes, is that because electrons, amoebae, and humans all do exist, they all exist according to what he calls 'the full power of existence.' Hence, although there may be higher or lower levels of health, wisdom, and intelligence, there can be no higher or lower levels of existence because, as he maintains, existence is never had at anything less than its full power. From this we are supposed to infer that there is not even a difference of degree, let alone of kind, between the instances of existence had by an immensely diverse range of individuals, between the full power of existence had by a human and the full power of existence had by a grain of sand.

According to Kenny and Hughes, not only would existence be utterly invariant as between different individuals but it would also be the thinnest, the most poverty-stricken of properties.[6] The existence had by Einstein or Aristotle would be neither more nor less than the pitifully thin existence had by a grain of sand. If that were true, there should be no prospect of saying anything more about it than has been said already in the earlier chapters. Both these arguments, however, are sadly wanting.

Reply to Kenny

Kenny's conclusion that existence is abysmally thin is supposed to follow from its being an attribute that is common to each and every individual. However, after noting that 'exists' can be predicated of mice and men, dust and angels, he would have needed some further premise like the following to ensure that his argument was valid:

> In any predication of the form 'b exists,' what the predicate 'exists' attributes to b bears no correlation to the kind of individual that b is. Rather, what it attributes is exactly the same no matter whether b is a mouse, a man, a speck of dust, or an angel.

No support has been offered for any such claim.

---

6. Munitz makes much the same point in his *Existence and Logic* (New York: New York University Press, 1974), 198. There he maintains that the parts of the world are '*qua* existents, *not different* from one another.' Emphasis in the original.

We might note, however, that existence is not alone in being common to different kinds of individuals, for the same can be said of intelligence, albeit in regard to far fewer individuals than for existence. It can be ascribed to dogs, dolphins, chimpanzees, and humans, and varies enormously even among members of the human race. Yet, from this it does not follow that 'intelligence' should be attributed in the same way to Socrates as to Fido. Although it might well be that the two uses of 'intelligence' do have a certain community of meaning, that will not serve Kenny's purposes, for their having a certain community of meaning fails to entail their having the *same* meaning, not even partly the same. Rather, it is equally consistent not only with their being partly univocal, but even with their not being univocal at all, for their community of meaning might be merely analogical (i.e., systematically ambiguous).

The fact is that the multiple uses of 'intelligence' provide no evidence at all for concluding that this property must be equally 'thin,' or equally 'fat,' or equally anything else on the scale between fat and thin. Rather, Aristotle's intelligence can differ vastly from Fido's or David's (a dolphin)—and not only in degree. Exactly the same point, however, can be made about Aristotle's, Fido's, and David's instance of existence: their mere multiplicity is no reason for thinking that they are any more invariant from individual to individual than are their instances of intelligence. Any argument for their instances of existence being uniformly thin, therefore, will have to be be grounded on something rather more compelling than the multiplicity of entities that have them.

It has also to be recalled that the ontologically basic element in the bound/bounded relation is not the bound, for the bound's actuality is parasitic on what it bounds. Hence, in regard to the actuality of Socrates, it is his instance of existence that is ontologically basic, and the bound—Socrates and all his properties—that is parasitic upon it. On the ontological scale, therefore, Socrates' instance of existence ranks decidedly higher than do any other of his property instances since, in being part of the bound, they are parasitic upon his existence in respect of actuality. Kenny would have been on safer ground, had Socrates been not the bound, but the recipient or subject of his existence, for then it would have been possible (albeit not inevitable) that his existence be as impoverished or as vacuous as he contends. Since, however, Socrates is not the subject of inherence of his existence but merely its bound, there can be no question of the instance of existence being impoverished, since the ontological riches lie not in any bound, but in what it bounds. The same can be said of any other instance of existence, even that of a quark. Hence, the answer to the question of how instances of existence rate ontologically vis-à-vis other property instances, is that they rate incomparably higher, since instances of existence are what is bounded, whereas all other property instances belong to the bound.

The second question was whether there would be any more than a merely numerical difference between various instances of existence. Now, although the richest property had by any individual will be its instance of existence, not all instances of existence will be *equally* rich—far from it. Arthur (an amoeba with all his property instances) will be a more restricted bound than Gerry (a gazelle with all his property instances), which in turn will be more restricted than Helen (a human with all her property instances). And naturally there would be variations from one amoeba to another, from one gazelle to another, and from one human to another. Speaking generally, therefore, the richness of an instance of existence will be directly relative to the kind of restrictions marked by its bound: an individual endowed with superior *kinds* of properties like intelligence, wisdom, and benevolence will have a bound that marks less restrictions than does one with less exalted kinds of properties. In the case of two individuals having the same *kinds* of properties, the richer will be the one with a bound marking the lesser *degree* of restriction on those properties.

Thus, Kenny notwithstanding, the richness and complexity of any instance of existence is in fact directly relative to what it is the existence *of,* and the range between the richest and the poorest instance of existence is immense. The modicum of truth in his contrary claim is simply that, if a mouse, a man, a speck of dust, and an angel all exist, then what is common to them is that each has an instance of existence. That, however, offers simply no ground for concluding that there is no difference between those instances, and still less that each is impoverished.

Reply to Hughes

As already noted, Hughes agrees with Kenny's conclusion, but for other reasons. His argument for the putative invariance between instances of existence is one based not on existence being common to each and every individual, but on its being an on/off property. To this argument the short response is that, like Kenny's, it too is simply a non sequitur. True, one can be more or less alive, more or less healthy, more or less intelligent, wise, handsome, and so on. Most certainly such properties are *not* on/off. Equally, existence most certainly *is* an on/off property: even though something may be only half alive or moderately healthy, it makes no sense to say that anything is only half existing or moderately existing. Thus, there can be no denying the truth of such propositions as 'Either *b* exists or it does not' and 'Either *c* exists or it does not.' Thus far Hughes' reasoning cannot be faulted.

Like Kenny, however, Hughes too requires a further premiss if his argument is even to be valid, namely:

> Whether it be in regard to *b,* or to *c,* or to any other individual at all, 'existing at full power' means precisely the same in each case.

Whether the required premiss is true is of course another matter. Consider, for example, two buckets, the base of each being fitted with an outlet valve that remains closed so long as water is pouring into the buckets, but which opens immediately when the pouring stops at any point *before* the bucket is full. Apart from when water is pouring into them, therefore, the buckets will be either completely full or completely empty. From their being full/empty, however, we cannot conclude that because two buckets are full, they contain the same amount of water. On the contrary, their being full/empty is quite consistent with the capacity of one bucket being two litres and that of the other being four. Similarly, from the fact that *b* and *c* both exist at full power it cannot be inferred that 'full power' entails the same amount of power *b* as it does for *c*. So, the further premiss would be false, and the argument for which it would have to be invoked is therefore unsound.

Thus, the answer to our second question is that the ontological worth of instances of existence can vary a great deal from one instance to another. The Kenny and Hughes arguments offered no evidence to the contrary. The evidence against invariance was simply that instances of existence have bounds that vary from one to the other not only numerically but qualitatively, for the less restrictive the bound, the richer the instance of existence that it bounds. Hughes was seriously astray in contesting the claim by Aquinas that 'a thing is more or less excellent according as its *esse* is limited to a greater or lesser special mode of excellence.'[7]

II. The Wealth of Existence, in General Terms

The question of whether existence is the most or the least impoverished of properties has already been answered, at least in very general terms. Indeed, the answer was implicit in recognizing that an individual is simply the bound of its existence. Compared with what it bounds, a bound counts for very little ontologically, as is strikingly evident in the case of the bound of a block of butter. The bound contributes nothing at all by way of butter or any other material. Similarly, in the case of Socrates and his instance of existence, the bound (the Socrates element) contributes nothing at all by way of actuality, whereas what it bounds (his instance of existence) contributes all the actuality. Since there can be no question of the latter being at all impoverished, therefore, all that remains is to spell out in what its riches consist.

This might be approached by comparing the discredited view that Socrates' instance of existence would have to inhere in Socrates with the view that it is bounded by him. According to the inherence view, Socrates' make-up—what constitutes him the kind of entity he is—would in no way be the ontological expression of his instance of existence. Consequently, 'Socrates exists' or 'Socrates has existence' would entail no more than 'Socrates is not nothing.' In other words, his instance of existence would be that by virtue of which he was something rather than nothing. In regard to his kind of entity

---

7. Aquinas, *Summa contra Gentiles,* Book I, c.28.

and to his nonexistential properties like being wise and being intelligent, however, his instance of existence would have no bearing at all on whether he was a man rather than a mouse, wise rather than stupid, and intelligent rather than dumb.

Likewise, to say that Socrates *receives* his existence would be to imply that he is in some way logically prior to his existence even in respect of actuality. In other words, even logically prior to being actualized by his instance of existence, he would in some way be already constituted as a human (with such and such properties) rather than as a mouse, or an electron. His instance of existence would therefore be totally irrelevant both to the kind of being he was and to the properties he had, for such matters would all have been settled, even logically prior to his receiving his instance of existence. Logically speaking, therefore, it would be too late for his existence to contribute anything at all to whether he was a man rather than a mouse or wise rather than stupid. Its sole contribution would be as an actualizer—actualizing Socrates and his property instances, ensuring that he was something rather than nothing. As Hughes would have it, 'the existence of a thing does not make it anything but existent.'[8] His instance of existence would be the same no matter whether he were a mouse or a man, a speck of dust or an angel. Had Socrates' instance of existence inhered in him, therefore, the views of Kenny and Hughes could hardly have been faulted.

Before evaluating those implications, however, let me introduce a distinction between what I shall call the ontological (or existential) content of the instance of existence as contrasted with the quidditative content of the Socrates element. To illustrate what I mean by quidditative content, consider a building. Since it is the embodiment of an architect's plan, we can distinguish the embodied plan from the materials that have been conformed to the plan. Considered in abstraction from the building (and from any surface on which it may be drawn), the plan has no ontological content (no actuality) whatever, but it clearly does have some kind of content. It is precisely that which I call 'quidditative' content. Again, consider an electrical circuit. Since it is the embodiment of an engineer's plan, we can distinguish the plan in it from the components (resistors, capacitors, transistors,

---

8. C. Hughes, *A Complex Theory*, 21.

etc.) that are interconnected in accordance with the blueprint. Here again the plan has no ontological content, no actuality (no existence in its own right), but does have some kind of content. As in the building case, this too is an example of quidditative content.

These two analogies may provide some insight into what is to be understood by saying that the Socrates element in a live Socrates has quidditative content. It has such content no less than does the architect's plan embodied in the building or the engineer's plan embodied in the electrical circuit.[9] Of course, the Socrates element has absolutely no *ontological* content, since its actuality is exclusively by virtue of the instance of existence. This is not to suggest that the Socrates element has no content whatever, but merely that the content it has is of a different kind, namely, quidditative.

Returning now to the implications of Socrates being the bound of his existence. The most obvious of them is that Socrates' instance of existence is logically prior to him in respect of actuality. Furthermore, being logically posterior to his instance of existence in respect of actuality, it follows (as noted in the previous chapter) that Socrates is not even conceivable logically prior to his instance of existence. The two points to bear in mind, therefore, are:

- Socrates' instance of existence is logically prior to Socrates in respect of *actuality*.
- Socrates' instance of existence is logically prior to Socrates in respect of *conceivability*.

From the first of these it can be said that the instance of existence is that by virtue of which Socrates is something rather than nothing. This is widely taken to be the sole role of the instance of existence. In fact, its role far exceeds so modest an assessment, for, as the second of our points indicated, the instance of existence is that by virtue of which Socrates is even conceivable as a human being, as wise, intelligent, and so on.

---

9. As has to be expected with analogies, the one I have drawn between the Socrates element and the architect's and engineer's plans does limp for, as readers would have noted, the building materials and circuit components are entities in their own right whereas the Socrates element is not.

This second role is as far in advance of the actualizing role as is the role of Mahler's third symphony in advance of the making of bare, undifferentiated noise rather than the making of great music. However, although the judgment about Mahler's symphony is hardly surprising, the judgment about Socrates' instance of existence is quite surprising, and represents something of a revolution in our way of understanding it. Hitherto, it may have been regarded as merely that by virtue of which Socrates was a bare, undifferentiated something. To have emerged now as that by virtue of which he was a fully constituted human being is striking witness to the fecundity of the paradigm shift in our notion of existence from being received by an individual to being bounded by it.

The Socrates element in a live Socrates has a very minor role indeed for, being merely the patterned bound of its instance of existence, it would merely mark the *limits,* the *reaches,* of the instance of existence, thereby ensuring that it pertained to Socrates and all his properties rather than, say, Aristotle and all his properties. What has thus emerged is that, although the ontological or existential content in a live Socrates belongs exclusively to his instance of existence, the quidditative content belongs exclusively to the Socrates element.

There is in effect no limit either to the kind of entities or to the kinds of properties for the ontological wealth of which instances of existence could not be responsible. The responsibility of any *particular* instance of existence would, of course, extend no further than the particular individual whose pattern it bears. Consequently, it will fall far short of exhausting the multitude of ways in which existence as such might in theory be instantiated.[10] All this is, of course, very general and needs now to be expanded in some detail.

---

10. Although perhaps tempting to do so, it would be quite misleading to conceive of an instance of existence as a limited or diminished form of existence *as such* or, perhaps, as one in which existence as such had been stripped of all but some of the ways in which it might possibly have been instantiated. To conceive of instantiation in this way would be seriously to misconceive it, for instantiation is merely a function that maps the universal existence (whether regarded as an entity or merely as a notion) onto instances of existence as values. Consequently there is nothing that it positively *does* to anything—not even to universals.

III. The Wealth of Existence, in More Detail

Since Socrates' instance of existence is the element in which lies all his ontological (as distinct from quidditative) wealth, we are entitled to have that wealth spelled out. At first sight, the task might seem to be merely one of listing all its properties. Yet, that cannot be right, for there can be no question of any first-level properties ever being attributed to Socrates' *instance of existence*. The reason is simply that his existence is itself a first-level property, and hence the only properties attributable to it are second-level ones like being common, or being rare, or occurring at least once.

Now, it is not difficult to see why any attempt to attribute a first-level property to an instance of existence can never succeed. The point is that, in attributing a first-level property F to an instance of existence (or indeed to any other first-level property), one must be able to form a closed sentence by attaching the predicate '___ is F' to the predicable '___ exists.' Clearly, that is impossible since the the resulting expression is '(___ exists) is F' which is not a closed sentence but an open one.[11] Unfortunately, open sentences attribute nothing to anything. First-level properties are attributable to individuals like Socrates or the Eiffel Tower, but not to property instances, not even to instances of existence.

This now poses a problem for, if the ontological wealth of Socrates' existence cannot—logically cannot—be spelled out in terms of first-level properties, just how can it be spelled out? Consider therefore the analogy of a light bulb through the filament of which electricity is flowing. Even if the current were in fact a necessary and sufficient condition of the filament's being *hot* and being *glowing*—which it is not—it would make no sense to attribute either property to the current itself and to say 'The current is hot and glowing.' There is, however, a related claim that certainly would make sense, namely,

---

11. That requirement is readily satisfied, however, when the property being attributed is a *second*-level one, e.g., the property of occurring at least once. In that case the attaching of second-level predicate '$(\exists x)\ (x$ ___$)$' to '___ exists' results in '$(\exists x)(x$ exists),' which of course is a closed sentence in which the variable 'x' fills the gap in '___ exists.'

'The current is that *by virtue of which* the filament is hot and glowing.' Much the same can be said in regard to Socrates' being intelligent and wise.

Although it is true that his instance of existence is no more to be described as 'intelligent and wise' than is the current to be described as 'hot and glowing,' it is also true that the instance of existence can be described as *'that by virtue of which* Socrates is intelligent and wise.'[12] Indeed, although the current has something to energize (namely, the filament), Socrates' instance of existence has nothing at all to energize, since Socrates is not something waiting in the wings to be propelled by an instance of existence on to the stage of actuality, as the filament is something 'waiting' to be heated by a current flowing through it. On the contrary, Socrates is merely the bound of his existence and, although the various instances of wisdom, intelligence, and the like can all be *attributed* to him as a bound, they can be attributed to him only by virtue of the instance of existence that he bounds.

Before developing this line of thought any further, I should dispel the suggestion that, even though the foregoing proposal has the merit of not attributing wisdom and intelligence to Socrates' instance of existence, it clearly does claim that Socrates' instance of existence is that by virtue of which Socrates is intelligent and wise. Surely that is tantamount to attributing to it the property of *being that by virtue of which Socrates is intelligent and wise,* and isn't *that* a first-level property? Not really. The objection would be valid only if the expression 'Socrates' instance of existence' were a name. It cannot be a name, however, for that would imply that his instance of existence was not a property but an object. What is it, then, if not a name? It is merely a nominalization of something like 'having Socrates' instance of existence,' much the same as 'wisdom' is a nominalization of the predicable '___ is wise.'

---

12. It is the nature of an analogy not be a perfect parallel but to differ significantly from that for which it is an analogy. An obvious way in which this particular analogy limps is that, although there can be a filament through which no current is flowing, there can be no Socrates that is not bounding his existence.

The proposition suggested by the objector has therefore to be understood as:

'Having Socrates' instance of existence is having that by virtue of which Socrates is intelligent and wise.'
or
'Whatever has Socrates' instance of existence has that by virtue of which Socrates is intelligent and wise.'

In canonical language, it can be expressed as

'$(x)(x$ has Socrates' instance of existence $\supset x$ has that by virtue of which Socrates is intelligent and wise).'

Although this does indeed contain two first-level predicables, clearly neither of them is actually being predicated of anything at all. In particular, the second of them is obviously not being predicated of the first. So much for this objection.

Clearly, although the instance of existence cannot be intelligent, wise, or any other first-level property, it certainly can be that *by virtue of which* Socrates is intelligent and wise. The riches of his instance of existence can therefore be conveyed not by listing any properties but simply by listing the virtualities that can be ascribed to it:

- That by virtue of which Socrates is *actually* wise, say, W_{sv}.
- That by virtue of which Socrates is *actually* intelligent, say, I_{sv}.
- That by virtue of which Socrates is *actually* benevolent, say, B_{sv}.

.
.

- That by virtue of which Socrates is *actually* Greek, say, G_{sv}.

The subscript 'v' is to be read as 'virtual' or 'that by virtue of which,' and the subscript 's' indicates that the virtuality is relative to a property of Socrates rather than of Plato or any other individual.

The list is but a small sample from the innumerable virtualities that might be associated with various instances of existence, and its membership matches exactly the list of nonexistential properties had by Socrates. For each of those properties his instance of existence has a correlative virtuality, as might be illustrated by figure 5.1.

Figure 5.1

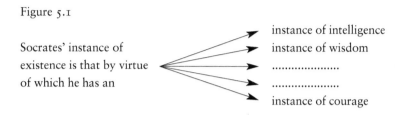

Socrates' instance of existence is that by virtue of which he has an
→ instance of intelligence
→ instance of wisdom
→ ....
→ ....
→ instance of courage

I use the term 'virtuality' rather than, say, 'what makes actual' or even 'what actualizes' since those expressions might suggest that there is already some entity to which the instance of existence does something, e.g., makes actual or actualizes. Prior to their being actual there is simply nothing that could be made actual. At first sight any suggestion to the contrary might appear to be answered by employing the de dicto construction, as in 'The instance of existence brings it about that (Socrates is actually wise).' Unfortunately, that too is misleading, since it suggests that the instance of existence is some kind of cause, which it could not be since it is not an individual itself but only an element in an individual. The term 'virtuality' or 'that by virtue of which Socrates is F' serves to avoid these misconceptions.

Notice that one and the same instance of existence is open to as many descriptions as there are listed virtualities. Notice, too, that the multiplicity of virtualities in the foregoing figure does not betoken any corresponding multiplicity or complexity in the instance of existence to which they are relevant. The point of listing all of W_{sv}, I_{sv}, B_{sv}, . . . G_{sv} is simply to underline the fact that each one of them is an expression of this single instance of existence. The simplicity of the instance of existence is no more impugned by the multiplicty of these expressions than is the comparative simplicity of a light beam impugned by the multiplicity of the objects that it illuminates. And just as the light beam is impervious to the spread of objects that it illuminates, so too is the simplicity of the instance of existence impervious to the number of property instances for which it is responsible.

As a caveat I should stress that, because Socrates' existence is that by virtue of which he is intelligent and wise, it does not follow that he is necessarily intelligent and wise. The reason is that, because Socrates is the bound of his existence and because it is quite accidental that the bound's quidditative content include being intelligent and wise, it is also quite accidental that his instance of existence be that by virtue of which he is intelligent and wise.

A further caveat. Having noted that instances of existence have no first-level properties, it might be suspected that a virtuality is merely a potentiality under another name. Certainly not. The distinction between the two can be explained in terms of a corresponding distinction at the logical level, namely, that between the de re and the de dicto uses of 'can.' I shall explain this by revisiting the claim 'Whatever has Socrates' instance of existence has that by virtue of which Socrates is actual.' Let us suppose that the relevant virtuality here really was merely a potentiality in disguise. In that case the claim would have to be understood as 'Whatever has Socrates' instance of existence has that by which Socrates can be (i.e., has the potentiality to be) actual.' Note that the use of 'can' is a de re one.

A Socrates with a potentiality to exist would plainly have to be one to which existence could accrue. To what, however, would it accrue? Not to a nothing, but only to something that had at least some actuality prior to any existence belonging to it. In earlier chapters, however, that proposal has already been dismissed as untenable. If, therefore, any sense is to be attached to 'Socrates can be actual,' it has to be one that does not rest on the possibility of any actuality 'accruing' to Socrates. That condition could be met by recognizing that the 'can' should be given a de dicto use, in which case the virtuality would be described as 'that by virtue of which it can be that (Socrates is actual).' This differs strikingly from the description of a potentiality as 'that by virtue of which (Socrates can be actual).' Virtualities, therefore, ought not be confused with potentialities. The temptation to do so stems from the ambiguity in 'can' as between two logical uses, one its de re use, the other its de dicto.

An objector might still hesitate to accept this conclusion. He might remind us of the scholastic tag *ab esse ad posse valet illatio* (from something's actually being the case one can infer that it can be the case) and suggest that, if it is true, 'Socrates is actual' should surely entail 'Socrates can be actual.' Not so. What it does entail is 'Either "Socrates can be actual" or "It can be that (Socrates is actual)".' To have eliminated the first of these options, as I did above, is not to have eliminated the second. Consequently, the admission of virtualities does nothing to violate the scholastic tag.

The account of Socrates' instance of existence that I suggest in terms of virtualities is a far cry from the naive view of existence as the most vacuous of properties, and likewise a far cry from the equally naive view of existence as invariant between 'mice and men, dust and angels.' In fact, it is far from invariant, precisely because his instance of existence has as many virtualities as Socrates has nonexistential real properties. Thus, the number and kind of those virtualities is the measure of its ontological wealth—the extent of its active power.[13] Similarly, the wealth of a quark's instance of existence is to be measured by the number and kind of virtualities which it exhibits. Obviously, then, the wealth of Socrates' instance of existence will differ enormously from that of a quark. It would be a grave misunderstanding to say otherwise, for that would mean that a quark's instance of existence had the virtuality of being a philosopher and of being a speaker of Greek, not to mention countless other virtualities all of which are in fact entirely absent from a quark's instance of existence. Speaking generally, therefore, there is no way in which the wealth of an instance of existence could be invariant as between mice and men, dust and angels. In the event, such a view can only appear quite bizarre.

Doesn't the foregoing account ascribe all the ontological weight to Socrates' existence? Indeed it does, for his instance of existence is that by virtue of which Socrates is not only something rather than nothing but also human, wise, intelligent, and so on. Of course, it could hardly have been otherwise, given that Socrates was recognized in the preceding chapter as being logically posterior to his existence in respect of actuality, a recognition that provided the impetus not only for the development of this chapter but for the preceding one as well.

As we have seen, however, it is one thing to deny the Socrates element any ontological role, but quite another thing to deny it any role whatsoever, for the quidditative role pertains to it no less entirely than did the plans of architect and engineer described earlier as

---

13. Powers may be distinguished into active and passive. Passive powers are merely potentialities.

embodied in a building and an electrical circuit respectively. That quidditative role is clearly indispensable and one not at all shared by his instance of existence. For one thing, it marks out which virtualities of existence characterize his particular instance of existence. For another thing, it individuates that instance, thereby distinguishing it numerically from all other instances of existence. Although these are admittedly not actualizing or ontological roles, they can by no means be dismissed as insignificant.

IV. The Critical Issues

Had existence been viewed as no more than an actualizer of individuals, there might have been a case, albeit no more than prima facie, not only for its carrying little ontological weight but also for its being invariant from one individual to another, from quarks to Aristotle. The critical issue for this chapter has been whether such a simplistic view of existence has anything to recommend it. Is existence really no more than an actualizer, no more than that in virtue of which an individual is something rather than nothing?

Had there been any way in which there could have been concrete individuals or concrete surrogates logically prior to their instance of existence in respect of actuality, the sole role required of it would have been to translate an individual that merely could exist into one that did exist—the possible into the actual. As argued in chapter 4, however, that view is quite untenable: neither individuals nor (concrete) surrogates are in any sense logically prior to their existence in respect of actuality. Quite the reverse.

This was the background against which the disputed question of the wealth or poverty of existence has been addressed. The answer to it lay in exploring the implications of an individual's being logically posterior to its existence in respect of actuality, i.e., being its bound, pattern, or imprint on its instance of existence. This, the prime conclusion of chapter 4, was without doubt the key consideration in rebutting the widespread view that existence must be among the thinnest of properties. Precisely because Socrates' existence was logically prior to him, it was not enough to say that it was merely that by virtue of which he was something rather than nothing—as if it were simply irrelevant to his being a man, wise, intelligent, and so on. Rather, there was nothing at all about Socrates to which it was not logically prior in respect of actuality, and that includes his being a man, being wise, and being intelligent. That is, it was solely by virtue of his existence that he was actually a man, wise, and intelligent. And that has put paid not only to the curious idea of existence as the most impoverished of properties but also to the equally curious idea that Socrates' instance of existence carries no more ontological weight than a quark's.

We have thus reached the end of a series of conclusions that were triggered by finding in chapter 2 that 'exists' was predicable of concrete individuals and, consequently, that existence was a property of them:

- The immediate question was 'What kind of property, Cambridge or real?' It would have been hardly surprising had it been a Cambridge property, but that is just what it proved not to be.
- That conclusion, however, seemed positively counter-intuitive since all first-level property instances—at least those other than existence—were parasitic upon concrete individuals in respect of actuality, and could be said metaphorically to 'inhere' in individuals. In regard to existence, however, the relationship was quite the reverse, with concrete individuals being parasitic on their instances of existence in respect of actuality, and being said metaphorically to be 'bounded by' their individuals. Recognition of the need for a paradigm shift from 'inhere' to 'bounded by' showed that the present difficulty was more apparent than real.
- The implications of the paradigm shift could hardly be exaggerated. For one thing, although it had been customary to ask rhetorically what existence might add to an individual, this turned out to be a question that could sensibly be asked only of property instances that were logically posterior to individuals in respect of actuality (inhered in them), but could not sensibly be asked of the property instance (existence) that was logically prior to an individual (its bound) in respect of actuality.
- It had also been customary to think of the role of existence as limited strictly to being that in virtue of which an individual was something rather than nothing. Because instances of existence

were logically prior to individuals (bounded by them), however, the list of their virtualities extended so far as being responsible both for an individual's being the kind of entity it was and for its having each of the properties that it did have.

- That, too, had some interesting implications for, as has just been seen, it disposed not only of the idea that existence was the most impoverished of properties but also of the quaint idea that Aristotle's instance of existence carried no more ontological weight than a quark's.

What began in chapter 2 as an exercise in philosophical logic to determine whether 'exists' was predicable of individuals has therefore proved to have ontological consequences that could scarcely have been foreseen. Through a series of conclusions each consequent upon the preceding one, an individual's instance of existence has proved to have an ontological significance and status that few might have suspected.

six

The Fullness of Being

It has emerged from the previous chapter that Socrates has nothing of ontological content except by virtue of his instance of existence. It would have been hardly surprising to find that his existence was that by virtue of which Socrates was something rather nothing. It was, however, entirely unexpected to find that his existence was also that by virtue of which he was a man rather than an electron and had all the properties that he did have rather than a completely different lot. It was almost as if the current flowing through a filament were not merely that by virtue of which it was hot but also that by virtue of which it was made of tungsten (rather than copper) and had the properties that it did have rather than some totally different batch.

At the end of the chapter it became clear that the ontological wealth of an existing Socrates was to be ascribed wholly to his instance of existence, and that it was to be described in terms of a package of virtualities.[1] If we compare two such packages—one with members ascribable to an electron's instance of existence and the other with members ascribable to Aristotle's instance of existence— it is obvious that instances of existence can differ enormously from each other in ontological wealth. In theory, they could be arranged in ascending order depending upon the virtualities ascribable to each. Reflecting on this series, then, one could speculate as to where it might be heading, what its terminus might be. There is an interesting

---

1. Remember that virtualities are not to be confused with potentialities: they are poles apart.

analogy—but only an analogy—between these questions and one that has been raised and answered by cosmologists.

A notion prominent among cosmologists is that of singularities, which are entities conceived of as points at which matter is infinitely compressed, and where the laws of physics as we know them cease to apply. When black holes collapse, they collapse into a singularity and, conversely, when the universe began to expand it is said to have done so from a singularity. For us, it is solely their infinite compression and the implications thereof that are of immediate interest. One implication is that a singularity has infinite density and, because matter is compressed to a point, it is also utterly simple. Each of these characteristics might prompt us to speculate whether there could be anything in the ontological scheme of things that was even faintly analogous to such entities in physics. More specifically, would it make sense to speak, even analogically, of any entity as being ontologically 'infinitely dense' and 'utterly simple'?

This is an intriguing conjecture, one that is encouraged by the conclusions of the previous chapter, in which the richness of instances of existence was found to vary immensely according as their bounds were less and less restrictive. Indeed, theoretically, there would be no point beyond which the restrictions could not be lessened still further, with a correlative increase in the wealth of the associated instances of existence. But, if at every point it was possible that there be a still less restricted bound and, correspondingly, a still richer instance of existence, could there not be some limiting case at which the bound would be eliminated altogether and the instance of existence be literally 'boundlessly' rich? Doesn't that point to our original question having an affirmative answer?

There are two reasons why it might not. The first is that a being in which all restrictions had been lifted would be one whose instance of existence was completely unbounded. Yet an instance of existence that was completely unbounded would be a property instance that belonged to no individual whatsoever, and that is a contradiction in terms—unless trope theory were true, which it isn't. It is for this reason that, although there may or may not be abstract entities that are existence as such or existence in general, there could be no *concrete* entity that was nothing but an instance of existence, for, although self-contradictory notions are perfectly graspable, they are certainly not instantiable in the concrete world.

Moreover, even if existence as such could, per impossibile, be a concrete entity, it would still be precluded from being even analogous to a physical singularity. The reason is simply that each of its properties would be distinct one from the other. Since the number of properties involved would be huge, such an entity would therefore be extremely complex. Precisely because of its complexity, it could be neither infinitely dense nor utterly simple. An entity has been proposed, however, which has claims to being both.

Unlike existence as such, this entity would be concrete rather than abstract. Like existence as such, however, it would be unbounded. Yet, despite being unbounded it would be utterly lacking in complexity, and eminently entitled to be described as 'infinitely dense.' I refer to the proposal for Subsistence Existence, an entity which has found support from the Jewish philosopher Moses Maimonides,[2] the Arabs Al-Farabi[3] and Avicenna,[4] the Italian Thomas Aquinas,[5] and many in the Thomistic tradition in later centuries. In their view, Subsistent Existence is an entity the essence of which is identical with its existence. They claim it to be God, and his being identical with his existence is central to what is called the 'divine simplicity,' according to which there is no complexity, no composition whatever in God, none between material parts, none between form and matter, none between essence and existence, none between essence or nature and anything to which it might be ascribed, none between genus and difference, nor any between individual and properties. These are all merely negative claims. Positively, however, the divine simplicity is said to mean that God is identical with his existence, his nature, and his real properties (though not, of course, with his Cambridge properties). Of all these claims the most basic is his being identical

---

2. M. Maimonides, *Guide to the Perplexed,* 2nd ed., M. Friedlander, ed. (New York: Dover, 1904), chap. 57.

3. R. Walzer, ed. and trans., *Al-Farabi on the Perfect State* (Oxford: Oxford University Press, 1985), 342.

4. *The Healing,* first treatise, chap. 6, translated by A. Hyman for A. Hyman and J. Walsh, eds., *Philosophy in the Middles Ages* (Indianapolis: Hackett, 1974), 240–62.

5. Thomas Aquinas, *Summa contra Gentiles,* bk.I, c.17; *Summa Theologica,* I, q.3.

with his existence, which is the reason for his being referred to as 'Subsistent Existence.' From it all the other claims are said to be derivable, including the apparently preposterous claim that God and each one of his attributes are identical with each other.

Unsurprisingly, the notion of a completely simple God has elicited widely diverse responses. Perhaps the most common is one of incredulity at the suggestion that his existence, knowledge, wisdom, power, and other attributes could be identical with God himself and, hence, with each other. For just that reason, some have dismissed it as incoherent, for surely it is quite impossible that his wisdom be the same as his mercy, or his mercy the same as his justice, or his intelligence the same as his power, and each of them the same as each other. How could those identities which are impossible in creatures be any less impossible in God? Such critics describe the doctrine somewhat unflatteringly as guilty of 'sophistry and illusion,'[6] and as failing 'to escape from a devastating atheological argument.'[7]

Not all proponents of divine simplicity, however, regard God as Subsistent Existence. Obviously, it would make no sense to say that he was identical with his existence unless existence were thought to be a real property of individuals. For just that reason the notion of Subsistent Existence has no place in the philosophy of Scotus and Ockham, neither of whom accepts existence as a real property of individuals, though each is a firm advocate of the divine simplicity. Nor, obviously, could Subsistent Existence be countenanced by those philosphers who deny that 'exists' is a first-level predicable and existence a first-level property.

Having noted the association between the notions of Subsistent Existence and divine simplicity, I shall pursue it no further for the moment, for divine simplicity belongs to the domain of philosophical theology. The notion of Subsistent Existence, however, belongs primarily to the domain of ontology, since it is concerned with the possibility of any entity being identical with its instance of existence or, conversely, with an instance of existence being identical with any

6. A. Kenny, *Aquinas* (Oxford: Oxford University Press, 1980), 60.

7. R. Gale, *On the Nature and Existence of God* (Cambridge: Cambridge University Press, 1991), 29.

entity. Whether such an entity would be divine is a still further question, one that it would be inappropriate to consider in a book that is not directly concerned with philosophical theology.[8] Whether divine or not, however, the notion of Subsistent Existence has been strongly criticized, as witnessed by the following passages:

A. Kenny: When Aquinas says that God is *pure* being, or subsistent being, he means that nothing more can be said about God's essence other than that God *is;* and this not because of our ignorance, but because of the pure and undiluted form in which being is present in God. But if we take 'esse' in the sense of 'life' or 'history' then the notion of pure being is as empty as pure life or pure history. There could not be a life which consisted of nothing but just living, or a history uncontaminated by anything actually happening. The attractiveness of this way of taking 'esse' was that it allowed us to conceive it as a rich totality rather than as an impoverished common factor. But if 'esse' is taken thus, then pure esse is a totality which has no parts, and its 'richness' is its entire lack of any property. *Aquinas* (Oxford: Oxford University Press, 1980), 59. Emphasis in the original.

C. Hughes: Although there is something more to Socrates than Socrates' existence, there is nothing more to God than His existence. In that case, it looks as though God will just exist, because there will not be anything else in Him over and above his existence, by virtue of which He could be anything over and above existent. Since there will not be anything in God but existence, and the existence of a thing does not make it anything but existent, God will be nothing more than existent.[9] But it seems clear

---

8. I have, however, considered it in *From Existence to God* (London: Routledge, 1992), and in *A Most Unlikely God* (Notre Dame: University of Notre Dame Press, 1996).

9. I might intervene to note that, in saying that 'the existence of a thing does not make it anything but existent,' Hughes is claiming that its existence is merely that by virtue of which it is something rather than nothing. As I argued in chapter 5, however, this is far from the whole truth, and ignores the fact that an entity's instance of existence is also that by virtue of which an entity belongs to a certain species and has certain properties.

that nothing subsistent could be just existent: a merely existent substance is too thin to be possible. *On a Complex Theory of a Simple God* (Ithaca: Cornell University Press, 1989), 21.

To the foregoing criticisms might be added those of Plantinga, whose immediate target is not the notion of Subsistent Existence but of divine simplicity, of which he considers two versions, one in which God is identical with general properties like wisdom, the other in which he is identical with *instances* of those properties. If formulated in terms of general properties, God would have to be a general property, merely an abstract entity. If formulated in terms of property instances, he would have to be a state of affairs. Plantinga regards either outcome as 'outrageous.'[10] Were he to apply his criticism of divine simplicity to the notion of Subsistent Existence, his conclusion could be exactly the same, for he could well argue that an entity that was identical with existence in general would be merely an abstract entity, not a concrete one. Similarly, if an entity were identical with an instance of existence it would itself be an instance of existence. Although it would be a concrete entity it would, alas, be only an incomplete one. Both outcomes might quite properly be regarded as 'outrageous.'

Kenny and Hughes reject the possibility of Subsistent Existence on the grounds of its ontological poverty. Kenny's claim that 'its "richness" is its lack of any property' is matched by Hughes' conclusion that 'a merely existent substance is too thin to be possible.' The objection I have derived from Plantinga is rather more basic, for it questions not the poverty of the notion but its very coherence. Its force stems from the fact that existence is essentially a property of individuals and hence is an incomplete entity. Subsistent Existence, however, is supposed to be a complete entity. It surely makes no sense to say that a complete entity could ever be identical with an incomplete one.

Clearly, two questions need to be addressed, and in the following order.

---

10. A. Plantinga, *Does God Have a Nature?* (Milwaukee: Marquette University Press, 1980), 47–52.

- Can there be any coherent account of Subsistent Existence?
- If so, what would be the ontological status of such an entity? Would it 'lack any property,' would it be 'too thin to be possible'?

Before addressing these questions, I should distinguish between two radically different ways in which the properties attributable to Subsistent Existence might be understood. One is as merely the *maxima* (limits simpliciter) of some properties had by creatures; the other is as the *limit cases* of such properties. In ignoring the relevance of limit cases, some philosophers, including the so-called 'perfect-being' theologians, have been severely handicapped in making any well-informed assessment of the notion of Subsistent Existence. My immediate task, therefore, is to explain the distinction between the limits simpliciter (maxima) of series as contrasted with limit cases.

Limit Simpliciter vs Limit Case

A basic difference between a limit simpliciter and a limit case is that the former differs merely in degree from members of the series of which it is a limit case: the limit simpliciter of a series of *F*s is itself an *F*. The *limit case* of a series of *F*s, however, is decidedly not an *F*. Consider, for example, the speed of moving bodies. As we are told, the upper speed limit is that of light. This is a limit simpliciter and it is a member of the series, albeit its maximum member. Although it might occur to us in an idle moment that speed has also a lower limit simpliciter (0 km/s), we should be wrong, for zero is not a speed at all. It is, however, a (lower) limit *case* of speed. Speed has no lower *limit simpliciter,* since there is no speed below which there could not be a still lower speed. An obvious difference between the lower limit case and the upper limit simpliciter of the speed of moving bodies, therefore, is that the upper limit simpliciter is indeed a speed (300,000 km/s) and hence a member of the series, whereas the lower limit case is not a speed at all, and hence lies outside the series of which it is the limit case.

First-level predicables provide a further example of this difference. They are expressions that can be attached to a proper name to form a proposition, and are often represented as having gaps which could be filled by proper names. Examples are '____ is wise,' '___ is

wiser than . . . ,' and '___ is wiser than . . . but less wise than _ _ _'.
It may be theoretically possible, even if practically useless, for them
to have any number of gaps. Purely for the purposes of illustration,
however, we might restrict the gaps to four, in which case we could
have the following series:

- 4-place predicable, 3-place predicable, 2-place predicable, 1-place
  predicable

A 1-place predicable is a limit not because its gap is not eliminable, but because any expression formed by eliminating that gap
would not be a predicable at all in a univocal sense of that term. One
could fill three places of the 4-place predicable, two of the 3-place,
and one of the 2-place, and in each case the outcome would still be
a predicable. We can see perfectly well what would happen if the gap
in a 1-place predicable were eliminated. In removing the last trace of
what makes an expression a predicable, the outcome would be an
expression that is not a predicable at all but an expression with a
truth-value, namely, a proposition. This is a limit case predicable
and, unlike the limit simpliciter, it is not a member of the series of
which it is the limit case. However, although not belonging to the series, it is not wholly unrelated to the members, since it is they, together with the way in which they are ordered, that *point* towards
this limit case: although different in kind from the series' members,
it is that towards which the ordering of those members does point.

Similarly in regard to a point: although differing in kind from the
ordered members of a series of shorter and shorter lines, it is that towards which the series points. Similarly, too, in regard to a line, since
it differs in kind from the ordered members of a series of ever narrower surfaces, but is that towards which the series points. Similarly
again in regard to a circle, since it differs in kind from the ordered
members of a series of regular polygons with ever more sides, but is
that towards which the series clearly points.[11] Thus, the limit case
of a line is not a line but a point, the limit case of a surface is not a

---

11. A polygon is regular if all its sides and angles are equal. Otherwise,
it is irregular.

surface but a line, the limit case of a regular polygon is not a polygon but a circle, and the limit case of a series of first-level predicables is not a predicable but a proposition.

It may now be intuitively, even if obscurely, evident what would count as a limit case and what would not. In an attempt to dispel some of the obscurity, I shall list the various series for closer examination:

- 4-place predicable, 3-place predicable, 2-place predicable, 1-place predicable. The limit case is a zero-place predicable, namely, a proposition.
- Regular polygon with sides turning by 360/3 degrees at its vertices, one with sides turning by 360/4 degrees, one with sides turning by 360/5 degrees . . . The limit case is a figure having no turning sides, namely, a circle.
- 1 metre line, .5m line, .125m line . . . The limit case is a 0m line, namely, a point.
- 1 metre wide surface, .5m wide surface, .125m wide surface . . . The limit case is a 0m wide surface, namely, a line.

About the first series it is clear that no *member* is either more or less a predicable than any other member, nor is any member of the second series either more or less a regular polygon than any other. Mutatis mutandis, the same can be said for the other series. In general, a series of *F*s is ordered according to the *degrees* of *F*-ness had by its members, all of which can be said to be an *F*.[12] It is crucial to recognize, however, that it is quite impossible for the *limit case* to be a member of the series of which it is the limit case, for it could be a member of a series of *F*s only if it itself were an *F*, which it cannot be.

What, then, is the basis on which the members are ordered? They are ordered according to variations in a defining characteristic. A defining characteristic of a first-level predicable is that it be attachable to one or more proper names to form a proposition. A defining

12. People differing from reasonably intelligent to brilliant can all be called 'intelligent.' Lines differing in length from one centimetre to one metre can all be called a 'line.'

characteristic of a regular polygon is that it be equisided and equiangular, of a line that it have length, of a surface that it have breadth. Note, therefore, that the first series is ordered according to variations in the number of proper names required to form a proposition with a predicable, the second according to variations in the number of sides or in the sizes of angles, the third according to variations in length, the fourth according to variations in breadth.

And what is the limit case in such series? In each one of them it is that in which the defining characteristic of the members has been varied to the point of extinction; and an F whose defining characteristic has been extinguished is not an F at all. In general, if there is a limit case to an ordered series of instances of F, there will be an *absolute* difference between it and the members of that series. It will no more be an instance of F than a rocking horse is a horse, or negative growth is growth, or a teddy bear is a bear. Consequently, the term 'limit case' in 'limit case instance of F' functions as an *alienans* adjective like 'rocking' in 'rocking horse.'[13] 'Limit simpliciter,' on the contrary, is *not* an alienans adjective in 'limit simpliciter instance of F.' Likewise, the term '1-place' in '1-place predicable' is not an alienans adjective, although the term 'zero-place' is.

To have understood the discussion of limit cases is also to have understood that the absolute difference between the member of a series of Fs and their limit case certainly does not entail that the relationship between them is merely a matter of convention. Clearly, it is not; otherwise, there could be no objection to allowing the limit case of a series of predicables to be interchangeable with the limit case of a series of polygons. Precisely this lack of interchangeability is our criterion for there being at least some kind of similarity, no matter how remote, between a limit case of a series and the members of that series. The similarity, however, will certainly not be a generic one.

---

13. As used in 'zero-place predicable' and in 'negative growth,' the terms 'zero-place' and 'negative' are functioning as *alienans* adjectives, which is to say that they alienate or change the sense of the noun they qualify. Thus, '"F" is a zero-place predicable' does not imply '"F" is a predicable,' whereas that is just what '"F" is a first-level predicable' does imply. Similarly, 'The economy had negative growth' does not imply 'The economy had growth' whereas 'The economy had fast growth' does imply just that.

I. The Limit Case Account of Subsistent Existence

Before embarking on the limit case account of Subsistent Existence, I should explain briefly the *limit simpliciter* account of God which is proposed by, inter alia, the so-called 'perfect-being' theologians who claim Anselm as their philosophical progenitor, though whether he would welcome their embrace is most unlikely. According to this view, God would have all the 'great-making' properties, namely, those properties which it is better to have than not to have. They are present in creatures at less than their maximum degree. In God, however, they would occur at the maximum degree possible.

In God, therefore, these properties would occur as limits simpliciter, and the difference between divine properties and creaturely ones would be merely a matter of degree, albeit of vast degree. No matter how vast the difference of degree, however, divine and creaturely properties would still be generically the same. Precisely for that reason, it would make no more sense to say that God's properties were identical with each other than it does to say that Socrates' properties are identical with each other. What would be nonsensical in regard to Socrates would be no less nonsensical in regard to God. As understood in terms of the limits simpliciter of property instances, Subsistent Existence would therefore be a bundle of contradictions, for it would be saying that the maximum degree of intelligence was identical with the maximum degree of mercy, which was identical with the maximum degree of power, which was identical with the maximum degree of justice, and so on. No wonder that perfect-being theologians will have no truck with Subsistence Existence thus understood.

I turn now to the main topic of this section, which is the limit *case* account of Subsistent Existence. I begin by recalling from chapters 3 and 4 that Socrates is logically prior to his instance of existence in respect of individuation, which is to say that the individuality of Socrates' instance of existence is parasitic on that of Socrates himself. In other words, in respect of individuation, Socrates' instance of existence is incomplete vis-à-vis Socrates.[14] In respect of actuality,

---

14. I call both Socrates and his instance of existence 'incomplete,' though not in the same respect. Socrates' instance of existence is incomplete

however, the converse is true, for Socrates is posterior to his instance of existence as regards actuality. In this particular respect, therefore, Socrates is parasitic on his instance of existence, i.e., Socrates is incomplete vis-à-vis his instance of existence.

Since there would be no such relations at all if there were no distinction between bound and bounded, our understanding of Subsistent Existence will be better served if we consider it not simply as an entity which lacks any distinction between bound and bounded, but as an entity which lacks each of the two incompletenesses that are correlative to the bound/bounded distinction. We need therefore to examine the implications of its lacking the following two incompletenesses:

6.1   Because it lacks any incompleteness in respect of *individuation*, Subsistent Existence obviously lacks an individuator, i.e., lacks any bound of an instance of existence.

6.2   Because it also lacks any incompleteness in respect of *existence*, Subsistent Existence might be regarded as lacking any instance of existence. That is to say, it might be regarded as a bound with nothing to bound.

At first sight, there would seem to be a striking incoherence about these claims. The immediate task is therefore to decide whether the incoherence is real or merely apparent. In so far as (6.1) is concerned, that will depend on how a zero-bound instance of existence differs from instances of existence that are *not* zero-bound. And that in turn will depend on how a zero-bound instance of existence is to be understood. In particular, is it to be understood as simply an infinitely expanded or enriched version of a creature's instance of existence, somewhat as the universe might be compared with an electron as being an infinitely expanding version of the very limited instance of matter or energy found in an electron?

---

in regard to *individuation*, since it is not individuated in its own right, but solely in virtue of being had by something that genuinely is individuated in its own right, namely, Socrates. Socrates himself is incomplete in respect of *actuality*, since it is solely by virtue of his instance of existence that he is actual.

I mention the case of the universe because both it and an elec-tron are genuine instances of matter, though differing from each other both in size and complexity. Is that how the zero-bound in-stance of existence is to be understood? Are it and Socrates' instance of existence both genuine instances of existence, differing merely in 'size' and complexity? If so, (6.1) would be claiming that a zero-bound instance of existence is not incomplete in respect of indi-viduation. Thus, (6.1) would indeed be incoherent, since it would be claiming that what was essentially incomplete (namely, an instance of existence) could in fact be complete. To decide that question, how-ever, we need to invoke the notion of a limit case that I introduced earlier.

Are Limit Cases Relevant to Instances of Existence?

Recall that the limit case of a series is that to which the members draw ever closer as their defining characteristic is progressively var-ied to the point of extinction. Thus, the limit case of a series of lines is that in which the length of the members has been progressively reduced to zero (a point), and the limit case of a series of regular polygons is that in which the angle through which the sides turn at the vertices has been progressively reduced to zero (a circle). Simi-larly, the limit case of a series of instances of existence would be that in which a defining characteristic of such instances had been varied to the point of extinction. We need therefore to consider whether instances of existence really can be ordered to form a series, or whether they defy being ordered. If the latter, the question of their limit case could of course not even arise.

Since a defining characteristic of an instance of existence is that it be bounded by an individual, our question is whether the various bounded instances of existence can be arranged in decreasing order of boundedness? The boundedness of Socrates' instance of existence, for example, is the inverse of the number and kind of property in-stances Socrates might possess. I say 'inverse order' because the bound of a grain of sand's instance of existence clearly marks more severe limitations on the virtualities of existence than does the bound on Socrates' instance of existence: the less an instance of existence is bounded, the richer the virtualities that are ascribable to it. So, when I speak of 'ordering instances of existence' in decreasing order of boundedness, I mean ordering them in increasing order of their virtualities.[15]

Of course, that could readily be done if the sum total of *nonexistential* property instances had by each individual could be arranged according as they restricted existence less and less.[16] But the difficulty with this proposal is that, even if agreement were possible on an ordering of individuals according to degrees of *F*-ness and likewise in regard to degrees of *G*-ness, agreement might be difficult in regard to degrees of the conjunctive property *F and G* (say, intelligence and musicianship), since there may be disagreement about the relative weightings to be attached to having *F* as compared with having *G*.

If there are difficulties when there are only two conjuncts, how much greater the difficulty if the conjuncts were to comprise the full range of real properties had by any individual. If there could be no agreement about *that*, surely there could be no agreement about the ordering of an individuals' instances of existence according as their bound is less and less restricting. But if there is no agreement about forming such a linear series, there would seem to be no sense in speaking of those instances as having any limit case.

While all this may be true, it is fortunately quite irrelevant to the question at issue, which is not whether any particular ordering can meet with unanimous acceptance, but whether any ordering at all (whether unanimous or not) is conceivable. What has to be considered is whether each of us could judge that individual *b* was more or less limited *qua* individual than *c*, and so on for all other individuals. If that can be done, albeit with much soul-searching and perhaps hesitation about borderline cases, then such an ordering is certainly conceivable. The ordering would of course not preclude the possibility of some individuals being *equally* limited. For simplicity of exposition, however, I am assuming the ranks to be totally ordered. An ordering is total if, given any two ranks, one is greater than the other. Otherwise the ordering is partial.

---

15. For the notion of the virtualities of an instance of existence, refer back to chapter 5, section III.

16. For the notion of restricting existence, refer back to the notion of the bound of existence in chapter 3.

Naturally, our ordering would reflect our own priorities and preferences, but so too would our rating of a list of musical compositions. Yet, those preferences do not preclude an in-principle ordering of the musical compositions from worst to best, though they may well preclude its being accepted unanimously. The point is that the notion of ordering individuals *qua* individuals (i.e., according to their being less and less limited) is no more questionable than that of ordering musical works, even though it may be incomparably more difficult. What is indeed highly questionable in either case is merely the notion of a *unanimously* accepted ordering.

I should add that it is not required that we be able to give an account of how we arrive at our ratings, nor that there be no hesitation or doubt about how to rate one or other individual. All that is needed for present purposes is that we know what it would be like for individuals to be so rated. The notion of b being more or less limited than c not simply in one respect, but *qua* individual, is therefore not a questionable one; nor is the notion of an ordering of individuals on that basis.

The Limit Case Instance of Existence

Given that the ordering of instances of existence according to their virtualities is conceivable, we might wonder therefore whether there is any point in an ordered series of decreasingly bounded instances of existence beyond which there could be yet another instance with a still less restricting bound. I raise that conjecture not to pursue it any further, but merely to stress that, even if there were such an instance (a limit simpliciter), it would never be a *totally* unbounded one. Consequently, it would differ only relatively—never absolutely—from members of the series of which it was the limit simpliciter.

Only a zero-bound instance would differ *absolutely* from any member of a series of bounded instances of existence. Yet, although differing absolutely from them, it would be precisely that towards which the ordered series points. For just these reasons, a zero-bound instance of existence would indeed be a limit case instance of existence. Moreover, even if there were total disagreement about the particular order of precedence among the series' members, the mere conceivability of *some* order of precedence guarantees that the limit case will always be the zero-bound instance of existence, no matter how the members might be linearly ordered. So, the notion of a limit case instance of existence is tenable, irrespective of there being any *unanimity* about the order of precedence in the series it limits.

It must now be recalled that, just as there is no univocity between 'polygon' in 'ten-sided polygon' and in 'limit case polygon,' so there is no univocity between the expressions 'instance of existence' in 'zero-bound instance of existence' on the one hand and in 'bounded instance of existence' on the other.[17] The zero-bound instance of existence could no more be an instance of existence than a circle could be an instance of a polygon, or a zero-place predicable be a predicable. And that is why, notwithstanding appearances to the contrary, there is merely an apparent incoherence in (6.1). Although it would indeed be self-contradictory to say that any instance of existence was complete in respect of individuation, there is no contradiction in making that same claim about a *limit case* instance of existence.

The same conclusion can be drawn about (6.2), for what has been said about an instance of existence that was not incomplete in respect of individuation could be said, mutatis mutandis, about a *bound* of existence that was not incomplete in respect of *existence*. Although it is part of the notion of a bound of existence that it be incomplete in respect of actuality, it is no more contradictory to speak of a (limit case) bound that is not incomplete than it is to speak of a (limit case) predicable that is not incomplete, namely, a zero-place predicable.

A zero-place predicable is not self-contradictory precisely because 'predicable' in 'zero-place predicable' has the alienated sense on which I have remarked more than once. Similarly, a limit case bound of existence that is not incomplete in respect of actuality is not self-contradictory, precisely because in that context 'bound of existence' is being used in an alienated sense. And just as 'zero-place predicable' referred not to a predicable but to a logical item in which there was no predicable incompleteness (namely, a proposition), so likewise 'limit case bound of existence' refers not to a bound of exis-

---

17. That is not at all to say that the two uses are totally equivocal, i.e., merely casually ambiguous.

tence but to an entity in which there is no incompleteness in respect of bounding. That, however, is just another way of speaking of a limit case bound of existence as bounding no instance of existence. Hence, (6.2) too is innocent of any incoherence, provided that the difference between the two uses of 'bound of existence' is not ignored.

Only One Limit Case Instance of Existence

Given that it does make sense to speak of there being a limit case instance of existence, we need now to consider whether there might not be more than one of them. This question might be thought to arise if the series were a branching one; it might also be thought to arise if there were parallel series of instances of existence, each series having its own limit case. According to the first suggestion, instances of existence would belong to the one series before splitting into two or more branches. According to the second suggestion, instances of existence might be considered as divided between two or more series having no members at all in common.

First let me say that the question of branching series or of parallel series might occur in the context of *evolutionary* series, and they are not my concern. I am concerned solely with a *conceptual* ordering. I therefore deny the need to consider the possibility of multiple series since, once it is accepted that instances of existence can be ordered conceptually according to their decreasing boundedness (or increasing virtualities), there is no reason to think that they could not be *conceived of* as all belonging to one and the same series.

However, let us suppose that, per impossibile, they really did have to be conceived of as forming multiple series. Any limit case of these series would have to be a zero-bound instance of existence. I say this because, as already noted, a limit case instance of existence could not be an instance of existence in any univocal sense of that term. Therefore, if any of the putative multiple series were to have a limit case (rather than merely a limit simpliciter), that limit case would have to be devoid of any bound, and hence would be a zero-bound instance of existence.

The question then is whether these multiple series would have the same limit case, the same zero-bound instance of existence. Let us therefore assume that they really did have a different limit case.

Then, to say that the limit cases were different would be to say that they were individuated, each of them being an individual instance of *zero-bound instance of existence*. But, to say that they were individuated would be to say that they were bounded, and that conflicts with the initial assumption that they were not bounded. So, the suggestion that there could be more than one zero-bound instance of existence is to be rejected as self-contradictory.

Subsistent Existence as an Identity of Limit Cases

Having cleared (6.1) and (6.2) of incoherence by explaining each of them in terms of limit cases, we might now consider the implications of their being *jointly* true. About Socrates we have been able to say that, in respect of individuation, he was complete vis-à-vis his instance of existence and, in respect of actuality, he was incomplete vis-à-vis his instance of existence. So, both the bound of his existence and the instance of existence that it bounded were incomplete, though in different respects. Now, the *limit case* of incompleteness in respect of individuation (i.e., the limit case instance of existence) has proved to be an entity in which there is no such incompleteness, i.e., one in which the existence has no bound. And the limit case of incompleteness in respect of actuality (i.e., the limit case *bound* of existence) proved also to be an entity in which there is no such incompleteness i.e., one in which no bound is actualized by an instance of existence. Clearly, an entity in which the existence has no bound is identical with an entity in which no bound is actualized by an instance of existence.

It has thus emerged that the negative claim of *lack of distinction* in Subsistent Existence between an instance of existence and its bound entails the positive claim that in Subsistent Existence the limit case instance of existence and the limit case bound are *identical*. There is thus no problem in maintaining that Subsistent Existence is an entity in which what exists = its existence. The reason is simply that the left-hand side of that identity claim is to be understood as 'the limit case bound of existence' and the right-hand side by 'the limit case instance of existence.' Hence, the claims translate into the following:

The *limit case* bound of existence = the *limit case* instance of existence.

This would be self-contradictory only if it implied:

Some bound of existence = the instance of existence which it bounds.

But, because 'limit case' is an alienans adjective, there is no such implication. The point is that a *limit case* bound is decidedly not a bound, and a limit case instance of existence is decidedly not an instance of existence. Consequently, there is no difficulty in maintaining that the very one entity is both the limit case bound of existence and the limit case instance of existence.

To sum up. The notion of Subsistent Existence depends crucially on the twin notions of a limit case and of a bound of existence. The first notion was developed earlier in this chapter, and the second in chapter 3. With the help of those notions, the frequently derided notion of Subsistent Existence proves to be derivable from the notion of any individual in the following very straightforward way.[18]

- Start with the recognition of Socrates as an individual that is related to its instance of existence as bound to bounded.
- Form the twin notions of the *limit case* instance of existence and of the *limit case* bound of existence.
- Note that the two notions have the identical referent.
- The notion of Subsistent Existence, then, is the notion of the entity which is jointly and identically the *limit case* instance of existence and the *limit case* bound of existence.

This, then, is the account of Subsistent Existence in terms of limit cases. It would seem to be innocent of the obvious incoherence that

---

18. Of course, it is one thing to derive the notion, but quite another to determine whether there is anything corresponding to the notion. My present concern is purely with elucidating the notion of Subsistent Existence, not with establishing that there really is such a being, a task that I undertook in *From Existence to God*.

is endemic to the account in terms of limits simpliciter, the straw man that 'perfect-being' theologians are so fond of deriding. The present account, however, has still to survive several other objections and misconceptions.

Misleading Notions of Subsistent Existence

Once Subsistent Existence has been understood in terms of the identity between two limit cases, it is not difficult to recognize the potential for being misled by such descriptions of it as 'pure existence,' or as 'pure actuality' (actus purus), or as 'the object that is identical with its existence.' As for the notion of pure existence, it might be thought to suggest an instance of existence occurring in complete isolation from any individual, belonging neither to Socrates, nor to Fido, nor to any other individual either. Such an entity would not be Subsistent Existence, an entity that is said to exist necessarily. Rather, it would be an entity which necessarily could not exist at all, namely, an instance of existence that was not the existence of anything whatever. On the one hand, it would not be an instance of existence unless it were existence of something; on the other hand, it could not be a pure instance of existence unless it were unbounded and thus not the existence of anything. Hence, the idea of arriving at the notion of Subsistent Existence by conceptually stripping some non-subsistent instance of existence of all bounds or 'impurities' is one that should not even be entertained, let alone pursued.[19]

The preceding point, however, seems to have escaped Keith Ward, who professes to think that the notion of a God who is identical with his existence entails that 'the sort of being that exists when God exists is simply existence.' This leads him to dismiss the notion with the comment that '"existence" is just not an answer to the question, 'What exists?'[20] This is exactly the kind of misrepresentation that has long both bedevilled and perverted discussion of Subsistent Existence. Although true in regard to nonlimit case instances of existence, it is completely irrelevant to their limit case. In regard to the latter, the

---

19. Equally to be shunned is the less tempting conception of creaturely existence as simply a contracted or bounded version of Subsistent Existence.
20. K. Ward, The Concept of God (Oxford: Blackwell, 1974), 157.

answer to 'What exists?' is certainly not 'existence,' but is rather 'the entity which is jointly and identically the limit case instance of existence and the limit case bound of existence.'

Having raised the possibility of being misled by the description of Subsistent Existence as 'pure existence,' I suggest that the danger is far from inescapable. Indeed, it is readily avoidable, provided that 'pure' is understood as 'zero-bound' and the existence in question is not thought to be something that is in any way *shared* with the whole series of instances of existence had by everything ranging from an electron to Socrates, but is understood as simply that towards which that series points, namely, its limit case.

Subsistent Existence has a long history of being known too as Actus Purus (pure actuality), which is perfectly correct, but which also is open to being misconceived, namely, as a being in which all potentialities are fully actualized. What is amiss with such a construal? Simply that no such being could ever differ absolutely from other members of the series of which it purports to be the limit case. Indeed, there could no more be an absolute difference between it and them than between a machine that never ceased operating to its full potential and one that merely *could* operate to its full potential but perhaps had never done so. Subsistent Existence or Actus Purus cannot be marked by any potentiality whatsoever, not even by potentialities that are always fully actualized. To say that Subsistent Existence is zero-bounded is not to say that all its potentialities are actualized to the full, but that it has *no potentialities at all* to be actualized. To say otherwise would be to deny that it was simple.

Although there is a perfectly proper way in which Subsistent Existence can be presented as 'pure existence' and as 'Actus Purus,' there is no way whatever in which it could ever be presented as 'the object that is identical with its existence.' Indeed, that would be as nonsensical as describing a proposition that has *no* proper logical parts[21] (e.g., 'Fulgură')[22] as an identity between a subject expression

---

21. A proper logical part of a proposition is any logical part of it that is not identical with it.

22. 'Fulgură' is a Romanian proposition that may be translated into the Latin 'Fulgurat' or the English 'It lightens' or 'It is growing light,' as one

and a predicate. Since subjects and predicates are logical expressions that differ in kind, it would have made simply no sense to say that they ever could be *identical* with each other. And it would have been equally nonsensical if, after contrasting 'Fulgură' with a proposition like '$(\exists x)(x$ is a dog),' the former had been described as one in which a first-level predicable and a second-level predicate were identical with each other, for that is precisely what they never can be. Mutatis mutandis, the same can be said about Subsistent Existence. To describe it as an *object* (in the Fregean sense) that is identical with its property (existence) would be absurd, since an object is precisely the kind of ontological item that differs absolutely from any property, and hence could never be identical with it. There is no absurdity at all, however, in denying identity between any *non*-limit cases (e.g., Socrates and his existence), while at the same time affirming identity between the *limit* cases, which is precisely what the notion of Subsistent Existence requires.

II. The Ontological Richness of Subsistent Existence

I turn now to the second of the questions foreshadowed earlier, namely, 'How rich would such an entity be?' Kenny and Hughes, who have dismissed the richness of an individual's existence as minimal, have predictably passed the same judgment on Subsistent Existence. Thus, Kenny has argued that, 'if told simply that Flora *is*, I am not told whether she is a girl or a goddess or a cyclone, though she may be any of these. But God's *esse* is *esse* which permits no further specification. Other things are men or dogs or clouds, but God is not

---

might say at the approach of dawn. The interesting thing about 'Fulgură,' however, is that it contains nothing corresponding to the suffix 't' in Latin nor to the dummy subject 'it' in English, i.e., nothing to which a *referring* role might be ascribed. On the contrary, it is neither more nor less than a verb stem, and hence contains nothing that could be construed as referring to anything of which 'lightens' or 'is growing light' might be predicated. For that reason it is an excellent example of a logically simple proposition.

anything, he just is.'[23] This accords with Hughes's contention that it would be 'too thin to be possible'. How compelling are these assessments?

The Wealth of Subsistent Existence, in General

Once an individual's instance of existence is recognized as *bounded* by that individual, its existence has to be accepted as more or less rich ontologically, depending on the extent to which it is restricted by the individual that both individuates it and marks its bound. As was argued in chapter 5, the less restricting the bound, the richer the instance of existence that is individuated by it. Thus Leonardo da Vinci's instance of existence would be incomparably richer than a speck of dust's.

Now, Subsistent Existence is the limit case of all non-limit case instances of existence had by concrete individuals. Moreover, their instances of existence are the richest of all their properties. As we saw in the previous chapter, an individual is merely the bound of its instance of existence, to which all of an existing individual's ontological wealth has therefore to be ascribed. We saw too that the instance of existence is far more than that by virtue of which an individual is something rather than nothing, for it is also that by virtue of which an individual both is the kind of entity it is and has the kinds of properties it does have. If even its instances are so rich, therefore, it is fair to say that their limit case will be not merely rich but the limit case of such ontological riches. Rather than being, as Kenny would have it, the ultimate in ontological poverty, Subsistent Existence would therefore be the ultimate in ontological wealth.

This is still a very general claim, for it is rather like knowing merely that John Smith is a billionaire, without knowing in what his wealth consists—whether in cash, in real estate, in stocks and shares, in oil wells, in manufacturing, and so on. Nevertheless, enough has already been said to rebut the ill-considered claim that Subsistent Existence would be 'too thin to be possible.' In what, then, does its ontological wealth consist?

---

23. A. Kenny, *Aquinas*, 58. Emphasis in the original.

The Wealth of Subsistent Existence, in more Detail

As noted earlier, Subsistent Existence would be the entity in which the limit case instance of existence = the limit case bound of an instance of existence. Since each side of the identity claim must have the identical wealth, it makes no difference which side we examine in detail, for the wealth will be the same even if the description of it may not. Because it will probably be easier to approach this by considering the wealth of the limit case bound of an instance existence, that is what I shall do.

Now, no property instances could belong to the limit case bound of an instance of existence unless they too were limit cases, i.e., unless they were zero-bounding. If it cannot be understood in terms of the *zero-bounding* property instances with which it is identical, therefore, it cannot be understood at all. To be more concrete about its being identical with zero-bounding property instances, let F_n, F_{n+1}, F_{n+2} . . . be property instances such that F_n is less constricting than F_{n+1}, which in turn is less constricting than F_{n+2}, and so on. Let F_0 be the zero-bounding instance of F, and hence the limit case instance of a series of Fs. The question then is not whether F_n, F_{n+1}, F_{n+2}, and so on could be identical with Subsistent Existence, but whether F_0 could. If so, how would that identity contribute to the ontological richness of Subsistent Existence?

Although I have not yet established whether any *non*existential properties at all do have limit cases that are zero-bounding, nevertheless we can say even now what the limit cases of some property instances would be like—should there prove to be any. More specifically, we might infer that, if there were a limit case instance of power, it would arguably be zero-bounding. The argument would have first to establish that power was what Aquinas called a 'pure perfection,' a property that was not *inherently* limiting. If power were such a property, there could be a series of instances of it, each member of which was less and less restricted. The limit case would therefore be one which was not restricted at all, i.e., one that was zero-bounding.[24]

---

24. If it were zero-bounding, it could not be part of any bound, for that would be to say that a part of a bound did not bound. So, the limit case in-

Assuming, then, that there really is a zero-bounding instance of power, how would it be related to Subsistent Existence? To answer that, let us recall the kind of relation that holds in *non*-limit cases, e.g., between Socrates' instance of power (P_s) and his instance of existence (E_s). Two points should be noted:

- P_s is a property instance which is incomplete with respect to Socrates as its individuator. It can thus be said to be completed by Socrates in respect of individuation.
- By virtue of being individuated by Socrates, P_s contributes to the bound of E_s. It can thus be said to be completed by E_s in respect of actuality.

Besides being completed by Socrates, therefore, P_s is completed also by E_s, albeit in a different respect. In regard to Socrates the completion is in respect of individuation, in regard to E_s the completion is in respect of actuality or existence.

So much for the *non*-limit cases of P. The point to be noted about its *limit* case (namely, P_0), however, is that, precisely because it is a zero-bounding instance of power, it could *not* be incomplete with respect to its existence. But, as remarked earlier in the chapter, what is not incomplete with respect to its existence is simply Subsistent Existence. Subsistent Existence would therefore be identical with P_0 or, as we may now call it, Subsistent Power. Subsistent Existence and Subsistent Power would be the identical limit case. They would therefore provide a striking contrast with the *non*-limit case instances of existence and power, between which no identity is even conceivable, let alone attainable.

There is nothing extraordinary about this identity between limit cases, for it is no part of the notion of a limit case that it be restricted to being the limit of just one series. Indeed, there is no reason why a series of Fs and a series of Gs should not have a common limit case. For example, a point is the limit case not only of a series of ever shorter lines but also of a series of circles of ever decreasing diameter. Hence, the mere fact of Subsistent Existence being the limit case

---

stance of power could be zero-bounding only if it were not part of any bound, i.e., only if it were not instantiable in any individual.

of a series of instances of existence is, in itself, no bar to its being also the limit case of one or more series of instances of other properties. And, in general, any property F which admits of a zero-bounding limit case would be identical with Subsistent Existence, and hence could also be said to be Subsistent F.[25]

It should now be recalled that being the limit case of a series of Fs means three things, all of which are obviously closely related:

- The first is that the limit case has at least *some* resemblance to the various instances of F in the series: if there were not even the slightest resemblance, there would be no reason for the limit case to pertain to a series of Fs rather than of Gs, or indeed of any other series.

- The second point is that the limit case is not a member—not even the ultimate member—of the series of which it is the limit case. Not being a member, the resemblance between it and the members must therefore be less than generic, and thus merely analogical.

- The third point is that the limit case must excel all members of the series not merely in degree, but absolutely.

These points have implications for the notion of Subsistent Existence as being identical with the limit case instances of all properties that are not inherently limiting. Thus, as the limit case of the series of instances of scientific intelligence of which Einstein's was a member, it would have an analogical resemblance to his intelligence. Mutatis mutandis, it would also have an analogical resemblance to Shakespeare's literary intelligence, to Michelangelo's artistic intelligence, to Socrates' wisdom, to Mother Teresa's benevolence, and so on. Moreover, the gap between them and their respective limit cases would be unbridgeable; and that is to say that Subsistent Existence

---

25. The very same conclusion might have been surmised on other grounds, namely, the a priori expectation that the relation between limit case property instances would itself be a limit case relation. Wittgenstein and C. J. F. Williams have argued that identity is not a relation at all. It might therefore well qualify as a limit case relation.

would excel them absolutely. Its ontological richness would thus be quite prodigious. Indeed, the mark of Subsistent Existence is not merely superiority but transcendence.

In answer to our earlier question, 'In what does the ontological richness of Subsistent Existence consist?' it has now to be said that Kenny was entirely right to claim that Subsistent Existence would lack all (non-limit case) properties. He was incredibly wide of the mark, however, in failing to recognize it as the common limit case of every kind of property instance that is not inherently limiting. To say that Subsistent Existence is *identical* with its intelligence, its wisdom, its benevolence, and all other pure perfections is simply to say that it is the *common limit case* of each of those properties.

Subsistent Existence would therefore be the entity in which all *zero-bounding* limit case property instances are united in being identical with each other and with the limit case instance of existence. For reasons mentioned earlier, the identity between these limit case instances is perfectly consistent with *lack* of identity between *non-*limit case instances of those very same properties.

An Objection

Some criticisms of the notion of Subsistent Existence rely on assuming that existence is not a real property of individuals. About them no more need be said here, for chapters 2 and 3 have laid that assumption to rest. Another objection, however, cannot be dispatched so readily. It was proposed by Prior in arguing that the notion of Subsistent Existence is quite unintelligible. Commenting on 'God is his existence'[26] being formed by filling the gaps in '___ is . . . .' with a concrete term ('God') on one side and an abstract term ('his existence') on the other, he condemns it as being 'just bad grammar, a combining of words that fails to make them *mean*—like "Cat no six".'[27]

---

26. In responding to Prior's objection, I use the term 'God' rather than 'Subsistent Existence' because that is Prior's own usage. The point could have been made equally well had he used 'Subsistent Existence.'

27. A. N. Prior, 'Can Religion be Discussed?' in A. Flew and A. MacIntyre, *New Essays in Philosophical Theology* (London: SCM Press, 1955), 5.

In reply, let me consider a series of property instances solely qua being incomplete entities. Thus considered, it is irrelevant whether the members of the series are instances of existence or of wisdom or of any other properties: all that matters is that they belong to a series of incomplete entities of varying degrees of incompleteness as in the following series.

- . . . 3-place property, 2-place property, 1-place property

Before saying more about this series, however, let us recall its correlative series at the logical level:

- . . . 3-place predicable, 2-place predicable, 1-place predicable

That towards which the logical series tends—its limit case—is an expression from which all gaps have been eliminated. By eliminating the last trace of what makes an expression a predicable, we get an expression that is not a predicable at all but an expression with a truth-value, namely, a proposition, albeit one that is logically simple in the sense of having no *sub*-propositional parts whatsoever, e.g., the Rumanian proposition 'Fulgură' mentioned earlier. This is a *limit-case* predicable: unlike a limit simpliciter, it does not belong to the series it limits, not even as its last member. I introduced the series of predicables because what is true of it is also true, mutatis mutandis, of the ontological series. That towards which the ontological series tends—its limit case—is an entity from which the last trace of incompleteness has been eliminated, namely, a complete entity.

Here, then, is a means of resolving the difficulty, raised by Prior, of finding a suitable gap-filler for an expression like 'God is identical with ___.' The problem was that it would have to be a complete expression, whereas it had seemed to Prior that any expressions purporting to refer to God's mercy had inevitably to be incomplete. What has emerged is that the limit case of an incomplete entity is in fact a complete entity, and the expression referring to it—'the limit case of a series of incomplete expressions'—is likewise complete. Consequently, although the proposition 'Tom is identical with his mercy' is ill-formed, 'God (the limit case of instances of existence) is identical with the limit case of instances of mercy' is perfectly well formed, which is exactly what Prior required.

III. The Analogy with Physical Singularities

I cannot leave this chapter without trying to dispel any lingering impression that it has been primarily about God. It has not; it has been about Subsistent Existence. True, there have been many pages in which God has featured, but that has arisen simply because many theists argue that God is to be conceived of as Subsistent Existence. In discussing their views on Subsistent Existence, therefore, one has little choice but to follow their example when they employ the term 'God.' My present concern, however, has not been with whether God is Subsistent Existence nor with whether Subsistent Existence is God,[28] but solely with explaining just how Subsistent Existence is to be understood, and how it would satisfy the notion of 'fullness of being.'

More particularly, I have been exploring the possibility, raised at the beginning of this chapter, of there being some form of existence that offered ontological analogues of two characteristics possessed by singularities in the physical world, namely, infinite density and utter simplicity. As proposed by its adherents, Subsistent Existence might well have seemed a likely candidate, for it has been described as an entity that is identical not only with its existence but also with each one of its properties. In view of those identities it could rightly claim to be utterly simple, for they leave no room for any complexity. Those same identities are evidence, too, of its infinite ontological density.

Against this proposal, the notion of Subsistent Existence has often been derided as incoherent. In the course of the chapter, however, it was noted that there were two radically opposed ways in which the notion could be understood. On the one hand, it could be formulated in terms of limits simpliciter; on the other hand, in terms

---

28. These are entirely different questions, ones which I have addressed in *From Existence to God*.

of limit cases. The former is a well-deserved source of derision, for it bequeathes us the insuperable task of trying to make sense of denying any difference between wisdom taken to its maximum degree and benevolence taken to its maximum degree, and the same for intelligence, mercy, justice, and so on. Try as one might, this simply cannot be done. Nor does it help to say that what is impossible in creatures might well be possible in Subsistent Existence. The point is that no concrete entity, whether Subsistent Existence or anything else, can be characterized by contradiction. Indeed, there can be no relief from the contradictions so long as the notion of Subsistent Existence is spelled out in terms of the maxima (limits simpliciter) of properties, including existence. So long as it is understood in those terms, the scorn directed at it will be not only inescapable but thoroughly deserved.

The alternative is to understand Subsistent Existence in terms not of limits simpliciter (maxima) but of limit cases, no matter whether the limit cases be of existence, of its bounds, or of any of the attributes ascribed to Subsistent Existence. Because there is an *absolute* divide between limit cases and limits simpliciter, what is true of the former may well be false of the latter. In particular, there is no problem about an identity between the limit cases of bounds and what they bound, nor about an identity between them and the limit cases of intelligence, wisdom, benevolence, mercy, justice, and so on. Thus, what is impossible in regard to limits simpliciter has proved to be eminently possible in regard to limit cases. And what would undoubtedly be a nonsense in regard to limits simpliciter can make perfectly good sense in regard to limit cases.

This chapter has therefore been devoted to explaining an interpretation of Subsistent Existence in terms of limit cases, to defending it against objections, and to removing possible misconceptions, especially the accusations of ontological poverty. A limit case of a series of instances of existence is immeasurably richer than any member of the series, and that is to say a great deal when one remembers from chapter 5 just how ontologically rich some of those instances of existence can be. Moreover, the limit case that is common to many different series of property instances is far richer still. Its riches would exceed absolutely those of any creature, even of one endowed with an astonishing array of eminent *non*-limit case property instances. There can thus be no question of Subsistent Existence being vacuous or impoverished.

It would, moreover, be the ultimate in ontological *density*, for the limit case of, for example, the scientific intelligence of Einstein, the literary intelligence of Shakespeare, the artistic intelligence of Michelangelo, the wisdom of Socrates, and the benevolence of Mother Teresa is not, as one might have thought, merely the ontological sum of five limit cases each distinct from the other, but is one and the same limit case to which those distinctions are entirely alien. At least in that respect it would be analogous to the physical singularities the notion of which helped to trigger the speculations of the present chapter.

This chapter began with the query what, if any, kind of entity could be described as 'infinitely dense' and 'utterly simple.' It ends by concluding that Subsistent Existence—the entity in which the limit cases of series of certain property instances are so to speak 'infinitely compressed' to the point of identity—could certainly be so described. Of all entities, it is the one that thoroughly deserves the title 'fullness of being.'

seven

Something of a Copernican Revolution

Anyone happening upon the dismissive remarks by redundancy theorists cited in chapter 1 might have been excused for thinking that debates about 'exists' and existence ought really to be a thing of the past. After reading allegations that the non-redundancy view stemmed from a 'bewitchment by language,' that it was the source of 'an almost unbelievable amount of false philosophy,' and that to take it seriously was 'parallel to treating Nothing as a name of a particular thing,' one might then have been quite startled to find any respectable philosopher claiming that 'the chief problem for ontology . . . is to give a satisfactory account of existence.'[1] Again, one would have been perplexed to find Geach being convinced that there is a first-level use of 'exists,' while Dummett was equally convinced that there is not.

Wherein lies the truth? The truth, as I intimated in the Preface, is that the alleged logical ascendancy of the redundancy theory has been the product of a combination of making false assumptions, asking wrong questions, and being oblivious to the paradigm shift needed in thinking about existence. What has emerged is that 'exists' is indeed predicable of concrete individuals, that it is indeed a real property, the richest of real properties, a property that takes an in-

---

1. M. Munitz, *Existence and Logic* (New York: New York University Press, 1974), 204.

dividual as its bound rather than its subject of inherence. In bringing this book to a close, then, I want to recall some of the principal elements that have led to that conclusion.

The foundations were laid in chapter 2 for, if the redundancy theory had been correct in thinking that all first-level uses of 'exists' could be proscribed, this book would have been stillborn. It was therefore vital to determine whether the impressive amount of evidence purporting to support such proscription could bear anything like the logical weight that has been placed upon it. That evidence was quite mixed, with some being theory laden, some theory free, and some stemming from fear that acceptance of 'exists' as predicable of individuals would encourage the idea that existence was a real property of individuals.

What might be called the 'theory laden' evidence was presented by those with a philosophical axe to grind, among them being Russell and Quine with arguments for the dispensability of proper names. If 'exists' were to be a first-level predicate, it should be attachable to proper names. If proper names were dispensable, however, there would be nothing to which 'exists' could be attached to form a proposition, and it could thus be reparsed out of the language. In rejecting this proposal, however, there was no need to contest its philosophical presuppositions, for the suggested reparsings of propositions like 'Socrates exists' proved to be untenable on other grounds altogether.

More interesting, but equally ineffective, were the theory-free objections—not only the familiar accusations of paradox and absurdity that were allegedly endemic to negative existential propositions but also the putative lack of any non-philosophical examples of singular existential propositions. Although the paradoxes and absurdities were widely endorsed in the twentieth century, they are so readily disposed of that, had one not known better, they might have been mistaken for trick questions rather than serious ones. The paradoxes were resolved simply by adverting to the straightforward distinction between a name's having a bearer and its having a reference. The absurdity was shown to be illusory simply by adverting to the equally straightforward point that from existence being a real property there could be no inference that nonexistence, too, would be a real property. Jibes about horticulturists examining several specimens of blue buttercup before concluding that none of them exist drew their force from this surprising oversight.

As for the alleged lack of non-philosophical examples, one might have thought that the embedding of 'Lord Hailsham exists' in 'Lord Hailsham might not have existed' and 'Lord Hailsham no longer exists' would have been acceptable evidence to the contrary. The ground for not accepting them has been to argue that the embedded propositions are no less subject to the paradoxes than the stand-alone use of 'Lord Hailsham exists' was thought to be. In every case, however, the putative paradox stemmed from a failure to distinguish between the reference of a proper name and its bearer. In addition to the embedded counter-examples, however, there were also such non-embedded cases as 'Joseph is not and Simeon is not' and 'Before Abraham was, I am' both of which were accepted as unexceptional English usage by the acknowledged masters of the tongue who produced the King James version of the Bible.

Although the question in chapter 2 of whether 'exists' was predicable of individuals was in the main not an exceptionally testing one, it did have to be settled before any discussion of existence as a property of individuals could even begin. It was in fact the launching pad from which everything else was to take off. The immediate inference to be drawn from it was that the reference of 'exists' (namely, existence) was a property of individuals. Still undecided, however, was the question of whether it was a real or a Cambridge property. Because there was little difficulty in showing it to be a real one, I shall not revisit the argument here but shall pass on to the rather more difficult, and quite pivotal, point concerning the kind of relation that an individual would bear to its instance of existence. Let me now recall why.

Although non-redundancy theories are not new, those in earlier ages seem to have been concerned primarily or even exclusively with establishing *that* existence was a real property. The question of just *how* that was possible—how existence would have to be related to individuals—seems to have been neglected. Perhaps the reason for the neglect is that unwittingly we have been locked into thinking of real properties after the model of wisdom, intelligence, and courage, all of which might be regarded as inhering in the individual that has them. As inhering in an individual, they look to it for their actuality, something that could scarcely be true of an instance of existence.

Rather, the reverse would be the case—an individual's actuality would be parasitic upon its instance of existence. This, however, so challenged the more usual conception of the individual/property relation as to cast grave doubt on whether existence really could be a property of individuals after all. Perhaps we had been too hasty in concluding that it truly was a real property. Perhaps it would have been more accurate to treat it as at best a Cambridge property. Or perhaps there was another possibility, one that did not conform to the paradigm exemplified by the individual/wisdom relation.

It emerged that there was indeed another option, one that was perfectly consistent not only with an individual being the individuator of its existence but also with its existence actualizing the individual. That relation was one for which an appropriate metaphor was not of existence inhering in an individual but of being bound by it. In non-existential cases, an individual had been *both* the individuator of its properties and their subject of inherence (and hence their actualizer). In the case of existence, however, these roles were split between the individual as individuator and its existence as actualizer. Like such properties as wisdom and intelligence, it was individuated by individuals; unlike those properties, however, it did not inhere in an individual but was bounded by it.

This represented a paradigm shift in the kind of metaphor to be employed in our thinking about existence, one without which it would have been immensely difficult to maintain that existence was the real property we had concluded it to be in chapter 3, and to conceive of its being logically prior to an individual in respect of actuality. That shift was in fact the turning point in the pursuit of an understanding of existence. From it virtually everything else was to follow, though that may not have been evident at first sight.

Although some problems had obviously been solved by recognizing that existence was bounded by individuals, it was not immediately clear whether all were. In particular, there still remained the challenge posed by questions like 'What does existence add to an individual?' or, in Humean terminology, 'What is the distinct impression from which the idea of existence is derived?' Such questions have been a running sore for defenders of the reality of existence, but one for which a satisfactory response has long been wanting. There are, however, at least two ways of meeting the challenge. One is to point out that, although it may make a great deal of sense to ask what a property adds to an individual in which it inheres, it makes no sense whatever to ask what it adds to an individual that is its bound, which is precisely the case with existence.

A second way of handling the questions is by exposing the contradictory assumptions upon which they rely, namely, the conflict between the following:

- Existence is commonly conceived of as that by virtue of which an individual is actual. That is, it is the notion of a property that is logically prior to an individual in respect of actuality.
- However, in asking what existence 'adds' to an individual, one must presuppose that there is an individual to which it may be added. In other words, one must presuppose that existence is *not* logically prior to an individual in respect of actuality.

Hence, to suggest that existence should add something to an individual is to suggest that it be *both* logically prior and not logically prior to an individual in the same respect, namely, actuality. Small wonder, then, that the question is unanswerable.

Although the bound/bounded relation was vital to the negative task of dispelling key objections to the reality of existence, it was equally vital to the positive task of understanding the role of an instance of existence. While people may differ as to whether *there is* any real property instance of existence, I suspect that parties on both sides have differed very little as to what a first-level property instance of existence would be like—if there were one. One has the impression that both parties would conceive of it as no more than an actualizer, that by virtue of which an individual was something rather than nothing, some individual rather than no individual. Recognition of the bound/bounded relation, however, has proved this to be a particularly simplistic view, though one that might well have lent a veneer of credibility to Kenny's claim that there was no difference between the existence had by 'mice and men, dust and angels.'

The actualizer view is merely a half-truth posing as the whole truth, and ignores the more remarkable implications flowing from the fact that an instance of existence is logically prior to an individual in respect of actuality. On an inherence view of existence, it might perhaps have been argued plausibly (albeit misguidedly) that an individual had at least some minimal actuality in its own right, even if only the *esse essentiae* espoused by Avicenna. According to the view of an instance of existence as logically prior to an individual, that conclusion is not even plausible. Rather, it leaves us with no option but to recognize that an individual has no actuality whatever in its own right but is completely parasitic upon its instance of existence. In the case of Socrates that means that his existence is not only that by virtue of which he is something rather than nothing but also that by virtue of which he is human, wise, intelligent, and so on.

From that fact it followed that the ontological wealth of an existing Socrates was not to be ascribed to the Socrates element—as is commonly surmised—but solely to his instance of existence. If the Socrates element has any wealth it is not ontological, but merely quidditative, the same kind of wealth as the plan embodied in a building or in an electrical circuit. As well, it followed that for every difference in the bound there would be a corresponding difference in what it bounded. Socrates' instance of existence would therefore differ from that of a dog, which would differ from that of a tree, and so on, down to that of a quark, and beyond. Across the whole gamut of concrete individuals, the differences between the ontological riches of their instances of existence would be immense. So much, then, for Kenny's contention that instances of existence had by these individuals would be completely invariant from one individual to another.

As evidenced in the following table, there is a striking contrast between the complex role of existence to which non-redundancy theorists are logically committed and the simple, and indeed simplistic, role of existence which redundancy theorists have held up to ridicule.

The Notion of Existence as Targeted by Redundancy Theorists	*The Notion of Existence as Proposed in This Book*
A. If Socrates had any instance of existence, it would be *no more than* that by virtue of which an individual was something rather than nothing.	Socrates' instance of existence is that by virtue of which he is something rather than nothing, *but, in addition, is* that by virtue of which he is human, is intelligent, is wise, is courageous, as well as all his other real properties.

B. Ontologically, the instance of existence would be among the *thinnest* of properties.	Ontologically, the instance of existence is *far and away richer* than that of any nonexistential property.
C. Qualitatively, there would be *no difference* at all between one instance of existence and any other, between Aristotle's and a quark's.	The ontological wealth of instances of existence can *vary immensely* from one individual to another.
D. Little sense can be made of the notion of 'fullness of being.'	Perfectly good sense can be made of that notion. Indeed, any entity that satisfied it would constitute the limit case of ontological wealth.

Clearly, the notion of existence against which redundancy theorists have chosen to rail is in fact a straw man, a mere shadow of the notion to which non-redundancy theorists are *logically* committed once existence is acknowledged as a real property of concrete individuals. It can be a real property only if it is related to an individual as its bound rather than its subject of inherence. And it cannot be bounded by an individual without being significantly more than that by virtue of which the individual is something rather than nothing. Indeed to have conceived of it in that way would be no less bizarre than dismissing the role of Mahler's third symphony as simply the making of noise rather than no noise. Thus conceived, the Mahler symphony would be as uninteresting as the sounds of children at play. Socrates' instance of existence would be equally uninteresting, if it were no more than that by virtue of which he was something rather nothing.

Of course, the truly fascinating thing about Mahler's symphony lies not in its being a generator of noise but precisely in what makes it so much more than a mere generator of noise. And the truly fascinating thing about Socrates' instance of existence lies not in its being an actualizer but precisely in what makes it so much more than a mere actualizer. Rather than being among the thinnest of his properties, therefore, his existence turns out to be by far the richest. And, rather than being invariant from one individual to another, the variation between instances of existence can be enormous.

Finally, let me return to the dismissive comments from Christopher Williams and Simon Blackburn deriding the suggestion that 'the idea of existence might be something deep and important' (Williams) or that Being might be 'a particularly deep subject matter' (Blackburn). They have presented the idea of existence as embarrassingly shallow, as the product of a bewitchment by language or as a 'parallel to treating Nothing as the name for something.' Damning conclusions? Not really, for what has become clear is that the object against which they have been inveighing is not existence at all, but merely a straw man of their own devising. The critics' notion has had to be turned completely on its head, to undergo something of a Copernican revolution, a paradigm shift in thinking about existence.[2]

---

2. Not entirely, however, for I have explicitly maintained that an individual is the individuator of its instance of existence no less than of its other property instances. I have also argued that the non-redundancy view is wholly consistent not only with an individual being a substance, but with its instance of existence being a property instance. At least in regard to these three key points the book is thoroughly orthodox.

Index

absurdity of negative existential
propositions, 24, 31–32, 163
Ackrill, J. L., 71
actus purus, 150
Albritton, R., 71
Al-Farabi, 133
Anscombe, G. E. M., on
individualized forms, 71
Aquinas, St. Thomas, 16, 113, 118n,
133, 154
on existence being received, 103n
Aristotle, 1, 109n
on individualized forms, 71–72
on 'inhering' and 'being a
subject,' 85
on redundancy theory of 'exists,'
10–11
atomic propositions, 4, 78n
attribution vs. addition, 106
Austin, J. L., 109
Avicenna, 14–15, 85, 133, 167

Bacon, J., 70n
Barnes, J., on the redundancy of
'exists,' 48–49
Bell, J. S., 92n
Berkeley, G., 12n
Bible, King James, 32
Blackburn, S., 2, 168–69

bound of existence
dual role of, 99–102
notion of, 97–99
Butchvarov, P., 104

Cambridge properties, 18, 38–39, 65
Campbell, K., on tropes, 70–71
categorial structure of the world,
67–69, 73
complete and incomplete entities,
4, 69
conceiving, distinct from imagining,
107, 109
concept expressions, 4. *See also*
predicates
concept horse, the, 8
concepts (Fregean), 4–5. *See also*
properties
concrete individuals, 1, 107
conservation laws, 92
constructional history of
propositions, 35. *See also*
propositions
contracting existence, 103n
contradictions, conceivable but
unimaginable, 107
Copernican revolution, 169
creation of matter, continuous,
93–94

170

About the Author

BARRY MILLER is honorary fellow at the University of New England, Armidale, Australia. He is the author of numerous books and articles, including *A Most Unlikely God,* also published by the University of Notre Dame Press.